Harvester of Hearts

Amelia Curran's oil portrait of William Shelley, 1819. The Carl
H. Pforzheimer Collection of Shelley and His Circle, The New
York Public Library, Astor, Lenox, and Tilden Foundations.

Harvester of Hearts

Motherhood under the Sign of Frankenstein

✦

Rachel Feder

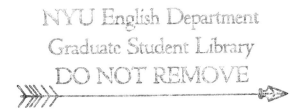

NORTHWESTERN UNIVERSITY PRESS

EVANSTON, ILLINOIS

Northwestern University Press
www.nupress.northwestern.edu

Copyright © 2018 by Northwestern University Press.
Published 2018. All rights reserved.

The poem on page vii is from Lorine Niedecker, *Collected Works*,
edited by Jenny Penberthy (Berkeley: University of California Press, 2002).
Reprinted by permission of the University of California Press.

Printed in the United States of America

10 9 8 7 6 5 4 3 2 1

Library of Congress Cataloging-in-Publication Data

Names: Feder, Rachel, author.
Title: Harvester of hearts : motherhood under the sign of Frankenstein / Rachel
    Feder.
Description: Evanston, Illinois : Northwestern University Press, 2018. | Includes
    bibliographical references.
Identifiers: LCCN 2018019341| ISBN 9780810137523 (pbk. : alk. paper) | ISBN
    9780810137530 (cloth : alk. paper) | ISBN 9780810137547 (ebook)
Subjects: LCSH: Shelley, Mary Wollstonecraft, 1797–1851—Criticism
    and interpretation. | Shelley, Mary Wollstonecraft, 1797–1851.
    Frankenstein. | English fiction—19th century—History and criticism. | Women
    and literature—England—History—19th century. | Motherhood and the arts.
Classification: LCC PR5398 .F43 2018 | DDC 823.7—dc23
LC record available at https://lccn.loc.gov/2018019341

For M & N

Who was Mary Shelley?
What was her name
before she married?

She eloped with this Shelley
she rode a donkey
till the donkey had to be carried.

Mary was Frankenstein's creator
his yellow eye
before her husband was to drown

Created the monster nights
after Byron, Shelley
talked the candle down.

Who was Mary Shelley?
She read Greek, Italian
She bore a child

Who died
and yet another child
who died.

     —Lorine Niedecker, 1964

CONTENTS

In the first stanza of an untitled poem from the 1960s, Lorine Niedecker asks two deceptively simple questions. One has an answer; the other does not.

Before Mary Shelley cast her lot with the radical poet Percy Bysshe Shelley, she was Mary Wollstonecraft Godwin, the daughter of feminist foremother Mary Wollstonecraft and the political philosopher and novelist William Godwin. While she never knew her mother and her relationship with her father was complicated, Mary Shelley's original name captures the essence of her literary influences. Indeed, it was her status as intellectual-historical royalty that drew "this Shelley" to her in the first place.

But who *was* she?

On election day, I called feminist literary critic Anne Mellor to discuss Mary Shelley and motherhood. We spoke in a moment of shared hope, on a day it seemed likely that the first woman would be elected president of the United States. But even as I played along, I knew otherwise. I'd woken with a tug in my gut, the place you used to kick me, the place that connects me to the greater fabric of the world.[1]

1797: Who was Mary Shelley when she rested in her mother's womb at her parents' wedding, or when she slipped from that womb, leaving Mary Wollstonecraft to die?[2]

Mary Shelley's names ask us to consider her, first as a daughter, then as a wife. But they also highlight the contours of her world, which was a world of ideas.

But Niedecker's first question rebounds in an echo chamber. It is also a question about the woman writer in history.

1812:   Who was Mary Shelley when her future husband and his wife, Harriet, came to dinner at Mary's family's home?

Twentieth-century feminist critics toiled to ensure that Mary Shelley would not be forgotten. They wrote books, edited tales and journals and letters. There were a great many women writers of the nineteenth century but something about Mary Shelley commanded this attention and inspired this labor—something about her life or work, her aesthetic or investments, her inherited names, her monsters.

In our conversation, Mellor stressed the difference between autobiography and life writing, explaining that *male autobiographers tend to think that lives have beginnings, middles, and ends* while a feminist counterargument suggests that life is *more random than repetitious, arbitrary*, that *lives don't have clear shapes*.[3]

1814:   Who was Mary Shelley when she "eloped with this Shelley" and traveled with him and with her stepsister across France, Switzerland, Germany, and Holland? When Harriet gave birth, in Percy Shelley's absence, to his son?

Rebecca Solnit describes books as "solitudes in which we meet," "a heart that only beats in the chest of another." She calls *Frankenstein* Mary Shelley's "immortal child."[4]

1815:   Who was Mary Shelley when she flirted with Percy's friend, with Percy's encouragement (he believed in a doctrine of free love)? Who might have been sharing Percy with her stepsister (we might never know)? Who was pregnant at the time, and had the child prematurely, and lost the child, and called Percy's friend to comfort her?

As this book unfolds, I survey feminist responses to *Frankenstein* and zoom in on specific engagements with Mary Shelley's work. In addition to interviewing Anne Mellor, I conducted archival research on Betty T. Bennett, the great editor of Mary Shelley's letters, who left behind a sprawling biography-in-progress when she died. I look at the power Mary Shelley held for the novelist Muriel Spark and for the groundbreaking critic Barbara Johnson. I also bring up exchanges with scholars of my own generation, including Romanticists Lily Gurton-Wachter and Anahid Nersessian, Victorianist Sarah Allison, and modernists Sarah Ehlers, Rebecca Ariel Porte, and Chet Lisiecki. "Mouth" is for Nan Z. Da, a scholar of nineteenth-century American literature and of Qing and early-Republic Chinese literature. The friend in "Taken" is Sierra Shaffer. This book exists in shadow form in hundreds of emojis sent to Stephanie Insley Hershinow, a scholar of the eighteenth-century novel.

In the poem "Alive Together," Lisel Mueller writes, "I like to think / I might have been Mary Shelley / in love with a wrongheaded angel, / or Mary's friend. I might have been you."[5] I don't like to think I might have been Mary Shelley, or think I could have married a man like Percy Bysshe Shelley or written a book like *Frankenstein*, or think Mary Shelley would want to be friends with me were we alive together. I cannot know who she was but I want to understand what she might mean to you and what she means to me.

1816: Who was Mary Shelley when she gave birth to her first son? When she traveled with Percy and with her stepsister in pursuit of the celebrity-poet Byron, with whom her stepsister had become involved? When their crew set up shop on the shores of Lake Geneva? When she started writing *Frankenstein*?

Who was Mary Shelley when Byron's personal physician was a little bit in love with her and maybe also a little bit in love with Byron, and wrote the first modern vampire narrative as a mockery of and perhaps love letter to Byron?

Who was Mary Shelley when her half-sister committed suicide and Harriet (pregnant) was found to have committed suicide and her stepsister was pregnant with Byron's child and she and Percy finally married and she and her father finally reconciled?

On the day of the presidential election, the most-searched issue on Google was abortion.[6] Texas has the highest maternal mortality rate in the developed world.[7] If I had been pregnant with a second child in China under the one-child policy, I shudder to think what I might have put at risk to have that child. Every birth story is also a story about reproductive justice.

1817: Who was Mary Shelley when she and her stepsister both gave birth to daughters and she finished writing *Frankenstein* and she published a history of her European travels, as her late mother had done?

Mathilda was finally published in the 1950s, edited by critic Elizabeth Nitchie from images of collected papers. Working directly with archival materials, Romanticist Michelle Faubert recently completed a new transcription, which will soon be published. In the current draft of her introduction to this new edition, Faubert calls the novella's reception "abortive from the first."[8]

1818: Who was Mary Shelley when *Frankenstein; or, The Modern Prometheus* was published in three volumes, when she traveled to Italy, where Byron claimed custody of her stepsister's daughter and where her own daughter died? Where she may or may not have adopted but not taken custody of a different child (we may never know that story, either)?

I read Lorine Niedecker's collected works from cover to cover during a verdant summer I spent working at a Vermont boarding school. There's a map of the Merck Forest & Farmland Center folded into my copy of the book, indicating sites such as "Burnt Hill" and "Sugar House." I thought warmly of Niedecker's long walks and simple day jobs and striking, minor modernism. I listened to Iron & Wine in my dorm room, never once imagining I'd sing the songs I was inadvertently learning by heart to my future son to help him sleep. I swam in the muddy water beside the canoe and rode a Clydesdale without a saddle.

Niedecker once wrote to the objectivist poet Louis Zukofsky, "The Brontës had their moors, I have my marshes." The poets' friendship "gave [Niedecker] direct access to the American avant-garde"; when Zukofsky got Niedecker pregnant in 1933, he insisted on an abortion. Niedecker later dedicated some of her most beautiful poems to Zukofsky's son.[9]

A palm reader once told me I would have exactly one child, while several doctors suggested that it might be impossible for me to become pregnant at all. Lorine Niedecker's untitled poem about Mary Shelley appears in a handmade chapbook she gave Zukofsky for Christmas.

1819: Who was Mary Shelley when her son died, and she wrote *Mathilda*—which Godwin would neither publish nor return—and then gave birth to another son?

Referring to recent abortion legislation in Oklahoma, one of my graduate students chirps sardonically, *we're just the hosts!*

Introducing her hybrid response to Hortense Spillers, Alexis Pauline Gumbs writes, "Again and again, there were phrases in her work that did far more than make her point. They made worlds."[10] Breaking these phrases apart and turning them, again and again, like the end words of a sestina, Gumbs invites me into these worlds, gives me a shot in the arm so scenes that didn't run through my blood run through my blood: "we are not born. we are made. (that's how we get played.)"[11] In an interview about the book, Gumbs offers a theory of love as praxis: "Love changes us. Love shifts our ideas of what is possible. Love, almost every time, causes us to restructure our lives in some way. Because of love, I sought a methodology that would allow me to write *with* Spillers instead of continuing to merely write *about* her work. The difference between *about* and *with* has to do with intimacy, conspiracy; maybe we can call that love."[12] In *Revolutionary Mothering: Love on the Front Lines*, Gumbs writes, "In order to collectively figure out how to sustain and support our evolving species, in order to participate in and demand a society where people help to create each other instead of too often destroying each other, we need to look at the practice of creating, nurturing, affirming, and supporting life that we call mothering."[13]

Who was Mary Shelley when she suffered a miscarriage that almost killed her? When a former servant blackmailed her husband over the child the Shelleys may or may not have adopted? When a second edition of *Frankenstein* came out, finally naming her as the author? When she wrote her fingers to the bone to support her only surviving son rather than relinquish him to an aristocratic father-in-law she'd never met? When she compromised with that father-in-law in her son's interest, if not always in her own?[14] When she edited her late husband's work and published so she would not perish? When she died in her early fifties and was buried between Mary Wollstonecraft and William Godwin?

Is the world we make in motherhood inherently a world in our own image, or can it be a new world? What about the world we make or reveal in literary criticism? I can view the past from my own perspective and pretend this perspective isn't a privilege. But if the form our work takes determines or predetermines the questions we ask and the answers we produce, can formal hybridity invite new intersections?[15] If I step into the frame, can I invite you in, whoever or wherever or whenever you are? In "Bewilderment," Fanny Howe writes: "Every experience that is personal is simultaneously an experience that is supernatural."[16]

Anne Mellor told me about her grandchildren and called Mary Shelley's only surviving child a mama's boy, which he probably was.

Harvester of Hearts

1

Forgetting

. . . a heart within that heart . . .

—Mary Shelley, *The Last Man*

You're never more yourself than when you're reading *Frankenstein*. The novel is a Rorschach test, a blot of ink, therapeutic. Assigning the novel is like running out for curry nine months pregnant and noticing who smiles, who chuckles, who averts their gaze.

As you watch the creature come together you take yourself apart at the seams. This is an exercise I perform often with college freshmen. They always side with the creature. They can't help it. He's poorly parented. Frankenstein just *ditches* him, passes out, forgets about him on purpose. They are the same age as Mary Shelley and they cannot help but sympathize. Even when they can't believe they're siding with the creature. Even when they say to the class, as if in apology, *it's not like I'm condoning murder or anything.*

Even when they say to me, before they realize they shouldn't, *you look like you're going to pop any day now.*

Mary Shelley knew as well as anybody what it was like to be a pregnant body. Her mother pretty much invented feminism, birthed her, and then died, so that kind of sets you up from the beginning.

On the topic, Barbara Johnson writes:

> Having a baby changed everything for Mary [Wollstonecraft], but she did not let that get in the way of her activity, nor did she subscribe

to the cult of motherhood that many other women endorsed. She treated pregnancy as an inevitable part of her life, not as an occasion for emotion. She did not consider it a solution to the problem of women's emotions, although her last novel is written fictionally to her (dead) daughter. In other words, Mary Wollstonecraft did not solve the question of women's emotion, but she did see motherhood as women's destiny. For Mary, this was certainly the case. She traveled to Scandinavia with a toddler from Gilbert Imlay, and she died of complications from giving birth to the future Mary Shelley.[1]

I have not solved the question of women's emotions, either. In this pregnancy, I have wept repeatedly from the same television advertisements. In one, for the Holiday Inn, a young couple with straight brown hair and rolling suitcases travels to a new town in order to adopt an infant. On the phone to probably no one, the future mother says, *we're nervous*.

In the timeline of Mary Shelley's life, there is at least one adoption, or possible adoption. Daisy Hay investigates:

> We know that at some point between December 1818 and February 1819 a female child was born in Naples, and that Shelley was either her father or felt in some way responsible for her welfare. We know that the child was not Mary's, although on the birth certificate Shelley stated that he was Elena's father and Mary was her mother. (Since Elena was left with foster parents in Naples this cannot be true.) We know that as a result of Elena's birth Shelley was later the victim of a blackmail attempt, probably because he lied on her birth certificate, a criminal offense. That he did so suggests that he felt it was imperative that the true facts of Elena's parentage be disguised. We also know that when Elena died aged eighteen months Shelley was deeply unhappy.[2]

We know so much about the lives of the Shelleys, and I am obsessed with how little we know about this. Theories abound, of course. Perhaps Percy had a child with Mary's pushy stepsister; perhaps Percy adopted the child to placate Mary's grief following the deaths of two of her children. But the truth has been forgotten. We may argue, in context, that it has been forgotten willfully.

I reread *Frankenstein* every time I teach it, and every time I read it, I am reminded that it is the great story of forgetting. Just as Victor continually turns away from his creation, choosing to be haunted by its shadows rather than facing what he has made, the novel itself contains pockets of quicksand, each disappearing into a different book, a book this book is not. The plots are holes we fall through. There's Justine's legal drama, like something out of the mystery novel that Mary's father invented. There's Felix and Safie's Orientalist romance, a jailbreak, a forbidden love. And there's Walton, our fearless frame narrator, out on his ship in the icy seas, headed toward the North Pole, recording all of this for his sister, Margaret, who may or may not ever get to read it. And in this world of monsters and mad scientists, sailors with secret histories and beautiful children, we get to be Margaret.

It's not easy being Margaret.

This morning when I woke up the baby was alert and curious, shifting under the stretched skin of my abdomen, finding my hand and pressing into it, jousting with the soft blade that my doctor tells me is his left elbow, the piece of him I know best, insistent particle.

Perhaps because I have fair skin and perhaps for no reason at all my belly displays a map of my child's desires.

The problem with pregnancy is that, much like a novel or the candlelit quiver of a late-night scientific discovery, it's a bad place to stop being yourself.

Jeffrey Jerome Cohen argues that the monster's body is a cultural body.[3] He uses Derrida to explain this but one could just use *Frankenstein*. The creature is a cultural body, literally—stitched together from fragments— and he enters into the world pure and childlike, a tribute to Rousseau, until everybody tells him, *you're a monster, you're a monster, you're a monster*.

The pregnant body is a cultural body, too. I could turn to the resurgence of abortion politics in America—it's a strange feeling when you realize that politicians suddenly care about your body, the little, fruit-filled body of an English professor hiking with her dog through the mountains, her future a tiny light under her sweater. You become public even when you're out there alone, like Frankenstein's creature pursuing him over the desolate and sublime landscape of the alps, except with an easy footpath and a view that makes you think of Monet's treatments of winter thaw. But the Shelleys didn't much care for the practicalities of governance and, although I do, I have a hard time feeling them in my gut. If we want to be small anarchists, better to talk about the fear machine inside my iPhone, which tells me everything can harm you, child, which tells me that, today, you are the size of a winter melon.

What can I know about the children of the Shelley circle, the tiny ghosts who haunt the pages? Mary's uncomfortable vegetarian pregnancies (her husband insisted, and she didn't exactly have great access to quinoa and kale smoothies), Shelley's son and daughter left behind in London? We know Mary's stepsister conceived Byron's daughter and it didn't go so well. I used to erase these children from my teaching; wasn't it sexist, I reasoned, to insist that Mary Shelley's art account for such quotidian losses?

Now, thirty-eight weeks pregnant, the whole thing just hurts to think about.

Johnson has a way with words, and with misery:

> Mary must have known at first hand a whole gamut of feminine contradictions, impasses, and options. For the complexities of the demands, desires, and sufferings of Mary's life as a woman were staggering. Her father, who had once been a vehement opponent of the institution of marriage, nearly disowned his daughter for running away with Shelley, an already married disciple of Godwin's own former views. Shelley himself, who believed in multiple love objects, amicably fostered an erotic correspondence between Mary and his friend Thomas Jefferson Hogg, among others. For years, Mary and Shelley were accompanied everywhere by Mary's stepsister Claire, whom Mary did not particularly like, who had a child by Byron, and who maintained an ambiguous relation with Shelley. During the writing of *Frankenstein*, Mary learned of the suicide of her half-sister Fanny Imlay, her mother's illegitimate child by an American lover, and the suicide of Shelley's wife Harriet, who was pregnant by a man other than Shelley. By the time she and Shelley married, Mary had had two children; she would have two more by the time of Shelley's death and watch as all but one of the children died in infancy. Widowed at age twenty-four, she never remarried. It is thus indeed perhaps the very hiddenness of the question of femininity in *Frankenstein* that somehow proclaims the painful message not of female monstrousness but of female contradictions.[4]

Fruitful ground, here, for a psychoanalytic literary critic. But Johnson leaves out something important—the sense that the Shelleys' marriage was, by all accounts and despite all odds, a damn good one. And that Mary Shelley seems to have been—in contrast to Victor Frankenstein—a pretty devoted mother.

Setting the monster aside: pregnancy is terrifying. Anyone who tells you otherwise is either lying, or a better woman than I am.

Addressing the connections between superficiality and monstrosity in *Frankenstein*, one of my students quotes RuPaul:

> *We are born naked and the rest is drag.*[5]

You are born naked, your head an arrow stretched thin by my efforts and pointed right at me.

I expected you fat and crying, but there's no soundscape in my memory.

Glossing Johnson, Judith Butler explains:

> there is some question about whether giving birth is itself monstrous
> or is intimately tied to a problem of monstrosity.[6]

For all those years, my students and I chastised the creator, his postpartum swoon:

> The different accidents of life are not so changeable as the feelings of
> human nature . . . now that I had finished, the beauty of the dream
> vanished . . . I threw myself on the bed in my clothes, endeavouring to
> seek a few moments of forgetfulness. But it was in vain: I slept indeed,
> but I was disturbed by the wildest dreams.[7]

Moments after your new skin touched my chest, I heard the nurse prodding me:

Rachel, Rachel, stay with us.

After years of wondering *how*, I myself fainted twice, clinging to you. I fainted from the blood loss, the hours of pushing, the days of effort. And as I woke, I thought, *just like in* Frankenstein.

I had a moment of understanding, but only a moment. Before long I was eating pancakes with my hands while your father held you in the window.

Today, I bind my belly in muslin. I listen to the new Adele album like the basic bitch I am. I stand guardian over your nap, contemplating my shrinking abdomen, my diminishing monstrosity, my screams a memory, the weeks between past and future buffering them like absorbent cloth.

What I'm saying is, you are my great story of forgetting.

2

✦

Channel

When my son got his first sunburn—right under his eye, a patch of skin I missed when I doused him with thick, mineral sunscreen—my stomach knotted up with "mom guilt." But who could blame me? Hiking the day before, we'd pushed to the point, the ocean crashing up against the cliffs, the elk languishing in their elk-ness, the pelicans rising and falling like stones, the seal—a seal!—spread flat above the water beneath us, too wide and still for my son to make it out in the bright light.

As my husband carried him ahead of me on the sandy path, I thought of the last time I'd visited this landscape. I'd been in Berkeley for an academic conference, had come up to Point Reyes with colleagues for a visit cut short by the conference schedule. I'd promised myself I'd return and make it to the point. These are silly things, stupid things—nothings.

During that conference, I became ill and needed to visit an emergency clinic for medication. I only told a couple close friends when I slipped away from the discourse and into my body. The medical technician who admitted me to the clinic was reading a paperback mystery novel, its spine broken, its pages butterfly-splayed on the table in front of him. He was incredibly comforting and something about the book itself felt comforting. In her commonplace book, Dorothy Wordsworth assembles a collection of poems and calls them "consolations."[1] Perhaps this is a lost genre of nineteenth-century women's writing, perhaps not. At the time, badly in need of steroids, my left eye dry and aching, I'd asked myself why literary criticism wasn't comforting, or, at least, wasn't comforting to me.

What I'm writing now isn't a consolation. A son thrives in your body by pulling the calcium from your very bones.

A poem of Mary Shelley's dated November 19, 1831, begins, "Alas; for Love! the gentle boy is dead!"; the poem goes on to compare its subject, a scorned young man, to "one of food bereft, / An infant orphaned by its Mother's care."[2] What exactly does this mean, to be orphaned by maternal care? Does this mean that, while the mother herself has not died, the care has, for some reason, been extinguished? So the boy, spurned in love, dies because he lost that love he relied upon for life, the love that was his birthright? Or does this mean that it is not the mother's death, but really the loss of care, that orphans the infant?

I have come to believe that maternal love is the source of all love. I know, I know! I know I'm insufferable when I talk like this.

In the period between 1815 and 1820, Mary Shelley wrote her most famous novel, *Frankenstein*, as well as its companion piece, *Mathilda*, a tragic incest narrative that was confiscated by her father, William Godwin, and left unpublished until 1959. During this same period, she gave birth to four children. When Mary Shelley wrote *Mathilda*, she had lost two daughters and a son and was pregnant with Percy Florence, who was to be her only surviving child.

For years, I asked my students to resist the temptation to read these texts in relation to Mary Shelley's life. My training in literary theory left me hyperaware of the problems attached to biographical reading, and my feminism demanded that students give *Frankenstein* the same philosophical breathing room they'd offer *Prometheus Unbound*. Instead, I'd present *Frankenstein* as a touchstone, a cipher, an origin story for contemporary culture. And I'd present *Mathilda* as its inversion, the monster now just a man.

When I taught *Frankenstein* and *Mathilda*, back to back, nine months pregnant, I had to rethink things. I rethought everything.

While not a consolation, this book is the document of my rethinking.

On February 22, 1815, Mary Shelley gave birth to her first child, a daughter. Either she was named Clara, or she was unnamed. While the Shelleys thought that Mary had been pregnant for seven months, Miranda Seymour and Daisy Hay deduce an earlier date of conception.[3]

Even now, a friend of mine lies in the hospital, the electronic fetal monitors throbbing against her abdomen, preeclampsia suspected, induction at seven months not ruled out. But things are so different now. I update my husband before bed.

It's early, I say.

He nods. *But not the end of the world.*

In a letter to Thomas Jefferson Hogg written on March 6, 1815, Shelley writes, "my baby is dead . . . It was perfectly well when I went to bed—I awoke in the night to give it suck it appeared to be <u>sleeping</u> so quietly that I would not awake it—it was dead then but we did not find <u>that</u> out till morning—from its appearance it evedently [*sic*] died of convulsions—."[4]

This is a book about reading literature like hovering over the crib waiting for the breath, letting the eyes adjust to the stillness until you notice the subtle rise and fall of the back, or a flaring of the lips as they suck in sleep, or the bringing of a hand into a fist. This is a book about observing without awakening, holding your own breath so you can be sure you hear. This is a book about maternal erasure, not only the criminality but also the intellectual profundity of it and the problems with that profundity. How's *that* for close reading?

Take that sticky "it." I mean, my god, not "she" but "it." That's new formalism and the new new formalism and, mark my words, the new new new formalism.

The journal from this period is different. The journal is heartbreaking: "nurse the baby & read Corinne" . . . "nurse the baby—read Corinne & work" . . . "I and my baby go about 3" . . . "nurse my baby" . . . "read talk and nurse."[5] Note this progression, from the baby to my baby to just "nurse," motherhood taken on and rendered invisible, the moving together like one person.[6]

In the days following the death, Shelley writes things like "still think about my little baby—'tis hard indeed for a mother to loose [*sic*] a child" and "stay at ho home net & think of my little dead baby—this is foolish I suppose yet whenever I am left alone to my own thoughts & do not read to divert them they always come back to the same point—that I was a mother & am so no longer."[7]

On March nineteenth, in her journal, Shelley confesses, "Dream that my little baby came to life again—that it had only been cold & that we rubbed it by the fire & it lived—I at awake & find no baby—I think about the little thing all day." On the twentieth she writes, "Dream again about my baby—."[8]

In her letter to Hogg, Mary Shelley continues: "& Shelley is afraid of a fever from the milk—for I am no longer a mother now."[9] I was texting with Anahid Nersessian about mastitis and she brought this up; she wrote, *I keep thinking of that line in Mary Shelley's letters, "Shelley is afraid of a fever from the milk"! Mastitis: Percy Shelley is ON IT . . . Only now do I see that, we may shit on Shelley for his trail of tears/dead children, but how many men know and care about mastitis? Even in the 21st century. Respect.*

Situating this moment of loss within a biographical account of Mary Shelley's flirtation with Hogg (her husband's idea, of course), Muriel Spark writes, "For many weeks Mary was haunted by thoughts of her baby . . . But since the death of her baby, a much more playful tone was introduced into her correspondence with Hogg, as if she realized that the time had now arrived when she must either become Hogg's lover—which she did not wish—or reject him. Mary compromised by investing the whole affair with a smoke-screen of flippancy, behind which Hogg might save face and vanity, and she make her escape."[10] I'm not sure I buy this interpretation, preferring to think the flippant letters to Hogg were Mary Shelley's Ben & Jerry's and *The Bachelor*, sentimental indulgence that erases what you're really thinking.

But what *can* we know about Clara? When I first told Lily Gurton-Wachter about this project, she wrote, *I was just mentioning Mary's baby who died yesterday in class actually, a detail which I've never mentioned in a class before, but now I can't stop thinking about it.* What does it mean to mention this baby—"it," "a detail"—in an 1815 letter to Hogg, in a 2016 classroom? What does it mean not to mention this baby?

Ellen Cronan Rose's 1995 article in *New Literary History*, "Custody Battles: Reproducing Knowledge about *Frankenstein*," surveys feminist responses to the novel:

Building on the initial assertion by Ellen Moers that *Frankenstein* is, despite its male protagonist, a "woman's book" that encodes Shelley's acute anxieties about maternity, Marc Rubenstein and Sandra Gilbert added that there seemed to be, for Shelley, salient parallels between procreation and literary creation. Mary Poovey and Barbara Johnson emphasized artistic rather than biological creation, but both took as axiomatic the autobiographical foundation laid by Moers. Thus, by the time Mary Jacobus wanted to excoriate Anglo-American critical practice for its naïveté, relative to French feminist theory, there was a well-established reading of *Frankenstein* available to illustrate her critique. All that remained was for Margaret Homans to recuperate the autobiographical, experiential elements of this reading by "translating" them into French.

This account of the gradual construction of a "feminist" reading of *Frankenstein*, while accurate in the main, has nevertheless elided what interests me most—anxieties internal to the production of feminist knowledge.[11]

Rose goes on to argue that, "In the genealogy I have laid out . . . there is a clear and systematic movement from the literal toward the figurative, from the material maternal body to the paternal symbolic order . . . Because her interpretation of the novel emphasizes biological reproduction, repudiation of Ellen Moers is one way for feminists to distance themselves from the maternal body."[12] Rose offers a cultural-critical take on this trajectory, suggesting that, "from the mid-1970s to the end of the 1980s, feminist criticism of *Frankenstein* assumed a shape that followed closely the contours of evolving feminist analyses of women's relationship to biological procreation."[13] She explains:

When feminist philosophers and popular writers alike saw motherhood as an impediment to women's achievement of independence, agency, and even full humanity, it was glaringly evident to feminist critics that *Frankenstein* registered a woman's highly ambivalent feelings about maternity. As (some) women gained access to technologies that enabled them to separate sexual activity from procreation, they ceased to regard biology as destiny. During these years—roughly from the Supreme Court's *Roe v. Wade* decision in 1973 to the mid-1980s, when radical feminist skepticism about the benefits to women of reproductive technologies began to percolate through the general public's consciousness—feminist critics increasingly distanced themselves from earlier autobiographical readings of Shelley's novel as they strove to display their mastery of the poststructuralist critical discourse that was current in the (still largely male-dominated) academy. When, for a constellation of reasons ranging from environmental to cultural, fertility and procreativity were revalued by (some) women as precious assets rather than impediments to full personhood, feminist critics began to revisit what Ellen Moers called in 1974 the "birth materials" in *Frankenstein*, this time to affirm the links between female sexuality and procreation and to criticize (male) science for attempting to usurp uniquely female powers.[14]

So our attitudes toward Mary Shelley and motherhood are determined by scholarly trends, on the one hand, and sociopolitical trends, on the other. Much like Frankenstein's creature, Mary Shelley's body of work is a cultural body, and her own body, from which that work issued and onto which we might ascribe some of that work's meaning, is a cultural body, as well. But what about her first daughter, the baby who died? What about that body, possibly unnamed, often unmentioned? What's the intellectual history of that small body, which looked like it was only sleeping? Or, perhaps more pertinently, is that baby part of my intellectual history, or Lily's, or Anahid's? Thinking about that baby's possible resting places, Bennett mentions that "the remains of deceased infants, either in a small baby coffins or wrapped in cloth, were laid by the sexton or an undertaker, for a fee, in the ground in the grave of a unrelated adult female without ceremony."[15]

I happened upon a blog in which a young mother was discussing the loss of a child. She wrote that all she wanted was to feel his arms wrap around her neck again.[16] That's stayed with me, and I think about it sometimes when I comfort my son. It occurs to me that my hug is comforting to him in large part because I am fully comforted every time I hug him. If his arms are wrapping around me, then I'm OK.

I've quoted Ellen Cronan Rose at such length because historicism is comforting, especially intellectual historicism that tells us why we're thinking what we're thinking. But something is left out here for me, too, what Goethe called—borrowing from a theory of chemical reactions—*elective affinities*. Is my elective affinity with Shelley—which, in contrast to Goethe's wine and water example, *changes* her, at least for students in my classes, or for whomever reads this book—the result of my "moment," replete with rising-star scholars tweeting about naptime and with, I kid you not, the prenatal belly dancing fitness class in which I met most of my "mom friends"? Or is Mary Shelley my mom friend in some deeper, darker way?

I'm not trying to be the literal worst, I promise. It's just that, in the months since my son was born, I've come to think of myself as a channel, the channel by which he and my words entered and enter the world. I finally understand Spicer, and Yeats, and Orpheus. The notion of the poetess as an "empty figure" and as "a medium for cultural exchange" feels less like a historically determined genre construction and more like a body part I've carried around forever but never really thought about—my gall blad- der, perhaps.[17] And all of this has to be about something more than the political aesthetics of motherhood two hundred years after Mary Shelley wrote *Frankenstein*. Doesn't it?

3

✦

Erasure

When I take my son to public places, there is a certain category of person who assumes that they are already friends with us because we are a baby. Today, for example, we visited a children's pool. Of course, my son cannot swim yet. He can't even crawl yet, and so I carried him in and out of the water and around the various water play attractions. A young girl with freckles named Juno accompanied us for some of the adventure, bobbing her goggled head in and out of the water.

Maybe twenty minutes later, we were having a bottle outside in the recreation center waiting area, and Juno came and found us. When I alluded to her recent experiences swimming with my son, however, her face became a small, blank image of disbelief. *How do you know?* She asked. *I was there*, I told her. *I was the grown-up holding the baby*. She blinked at me, sweet and completely sincere. *I still don't remember you*, she confessed.

This brings us to the topic of maternal erasure.

I always tell people *Mathilda* is Mary Shelley's incest narrative, but that's not really what it's about, or, at least, that's not all it's about. Rereading the novella a couple months after my son's birth, I found myself paying little attention to the scandal. Instead, I finally saw all the mothers the novella edits out. When the father's mother dies, he marries Diana. When Mathilda is born, Diana dies. When the father is consumed by forbidden passion, he tries to relive Diana's death, returning to the home he shared with her, her pages still earmarked.

Later, after the confession and the tragedy, after Mathilda fakes her own death and retires to a secluded cottage on the heath, after "a fox came every day for a portion of food appropriated for him and would suffer me to pat his head,"[1] after I reread this book outside my own cottage in the foothills, not yet pregnant, and looked up to see a fox watching me, just feet away, Mathilda asks her friend, the poet Woodville, to die with her. Woodville says, "Indeed I dare not die. I have a mother whose support and hope I am."[2] When this mother becomes ill, Woodville departs; that's when Mathilda finally dies.

Critics tend to read the characters biographically. Diana would be Mary Wollstonecraft. ("I was born, and my mother died a few days after my birth."[3]) Godwin's confiscation of the manuscript, his refusal to either publish or return it, adds fuel to the fire. Terence Harpold writes:

> *Mathilda* represents a fantasy of seduction, Mary's refiguring of the scene of her origin, subject to the effects of the father's intervention in mother-daughter identifications . . . The submission of the novel to Godwin signals Mary's effort to engage him in the seduction fantasy, but to acknowledge the authority of his desire in the primal scene which determines her understanding of herself and her relations with each of her parents. The daughter's need to acknowledge the father's authority is brought to crisis by the loss of the son whose name had previously signified that authority [William Shelley] . . . Mary submits the manuscript through Maria [Gisborne], who, acting in the place of the idealized mother (for both the daughter and the father), figures the fantasy mother's acquiescence to the daughter's succession to the mother's place . . . The loss of William requires a substitute sign of submission to the father's desire—the manuscript of *Mathilda*.[4]

This was back in 1989, of course, the year my brother was born, when one could get away with publishing such a thing, its aches and balances, its map of the heart.[5]

And what of the history I am writing?

Mary Shelley wrote *Mathilda* after *Frankenstein* and following the deaths of three children. She was pregnant, we should note, with Percy Florence, who was to be her only surviving child.

At that moment, what must motherhood have seemed like to Mary Shelley? An impossible inevitability? An embodied absence? In 1815, after waking to find her first child dead, Shelley wrote, "I was a mother & am so no longer."[6] It's possibly the saddest ampersand in all of English letters, a connective knot that unravels, attaches to nothing. And it's a history that repeated itself, at least for Mary.

In a letter to Marianne Hunt, written after Percy Florence was born, Mary Shelley describes her months of being childless:

> he is my only one and although he is so healthy and promising that for the life of me I cannot fear yet it is a bitter thought that all should be risked on one yet how much sweeter than to be childless as I was for 5 hateful months—Do not lett [*sic*] us talk of those five months: when I look back on all I suffered at Leghorn I shudder with horror yet even now a sickening feeling steps in the way of every enjoyment when I think—of what I will not write about.[7]

Lily, who brought this passage to my attention, said it struck her as *a strange thing to say, as though the value is in having a child at all rather than any particular child.*

As far as we know, those "hateful months" include the period when Mary Shelley wrote *Mathilda*, which shares the letter's strange mathematics. The tragedy of *Mathilda* comes about because Mathilda only has her father, and because her father only has her. Glossing this, Lily said, *you could risk only loving one person but when that one person is your father then you are, as Mathilda says,* "in love with death."[8]

When I was pregnant, a friend told me that, for her, the weirdest part of childbirth was going into the hospital as one person and coming out as two people. When I told this to Lily, she reminded me that being pregnant is being yourself and also being someone else. So is motherhood a question of addition and multiplication, or of division and subtraction?

Anne Mellor writes, "Mathilda's inability to imagine an adult life in society for herself is partly caused by the absence of her mother . . . both Mary Shelley and Mathilda reenact the psychological drama of the mother-daughter relationship in a typical father-daughter incest family, one in which the daughter experiences her mother as absent."[9] I want to understand the difference between *absent* and *erased*.

In *Mathilda*, a neglected child is driven by a compulsion she can't quite explain to determine her father's secret, which turns out to be, spoiler alert, his incestuous desire for her. The scene is eerily reminiscent of

Godwin's Caleb Williams pushing for Falkland's murderous confession. If Godwin invented the mystery novel (or, at least, didn't *not* invent it), then *Mathilda* is its child, a purely psychological thriller, its ingénue sleuth pressing for a sin that exists only as an idea.

When I visited campus before starting my job, I met a graduate student (now a professor) who was writing a novel on fathers and daughters. In the novel, the father in question is a professor of fatherhood studies.[10] I told her to read *Mathilda*, of course, although I don't want to read the novella in the context of fatherhood studies. What I'd like to do, instead, is to use *Mathilda* as an occasion to invent a motherhood studies comprised of reading as a mother for the mothers who are missing.

I was a mother & am so no longer. I was a mother & am a mother no longer. I am no longer a mother and thus no longer am. The loss of the child a loss of the self so complete, so much better than the modernists could imagine.

I teach Mary Wollstonecraft's unfinished novel, *The Wrongs of Woman, or Maria*, for the first time six months after giving birth. One of my students has come to class prepared with a list of reasons why women were confined to mental institutions in the late eighteenth and early nineteenth centuries. In the case of Maria, society punishes a mother for nonconformity. She tries but fails to protect her child. She escapes an unhealthy family situation into an abusive marriage, then tries to escape that marriage. As in *Caleb Williams*, the villain, in this case her husband, cannot let her go, and hunts her out. She is drugged and wakes up in a private madhouse, separated from her four-month-old daughter. Eventually she wins the confidence of an asylum employee, Jemima, also a victim of abuse and neglect. Jemima sets out from the asylum for information, and must tell Maria that her daughter has died. She does this with silence.

The day after I teach *Maria*, I'm feeling panicky. I can't put my finger on the reason why. I don't want my husband to take the baby for lunch with his colleagues. I feel a diluted fear tinge the air.

He wants to eat buttons, my husband explains from the sofa. The baby has been tugging at his shirt.

He cannot, I reply.

One must start *Maria* at the end, where it dissolves. Editing the novella after Wollstonecraft's death, Godwin writes, "VERY few hints exist respecting the plan of the remainder of the work. I find only two detached sentences, and some scattered heads for the continuation of the story. I transcribe the whole."[11]

The remainder of the text reads like those choose-your-own-adventure *Goosebumps* books one used to devour on sun-warmed concrete under a fort constructed of damp pool towels and folding chairs, albeit darker or, at least, more explicit about its darkness. "Trial for adultery . . . Once more pregnant . . . Consequence . . . Sued . . . A miscarriage . . . Suicide." There's one happy ending, the daughter found alive, the news of her death malignant misinformation, Maria exclaiming, "I will live for my child!"[12]

But the swell of relief I feel (now that I'm a mother, I'm such a sentimental reader) is soon overtaken by a sickening feeling as I remember the irony. The novel is unfinished because Mary Wollstonecraft died eleven days after giving birth to her daughter. She couldn't expel the placenta, and a doctor with dirty hands pulled it out piece by piece, causing an infection.[13] (In the novel, Jemima's mother dies nine days after her birth, leaving her "consigned to the care of the cheapest nurse my father could find" and altogether cast out into a world that will not care for her.)[14]

It almost feels embarrassing to use phrases like "swell of relief" and "sickening feeling." I'm a scholar, after all. Barthes has taught us that the author is dead, New Criticism has insisted that I read in a vacuum, Stanley Fish has yelled at me about trespassing the boundaries of critique (on which more later). Literary criticism insists on argumentative intervention as the gold standard of analysis, a masculinist norm that holds little space for the author's placenta. (Think of a myth of Sappho, fragments pulled from the husk of an alligator.)

But I read differently now. Nearly forty hours passed between the time my water broke in the British and Irish Studies Reading Room and the time my son left my body and entered the world. I have a vague memory of drifting in and out of consciousness while the doctor pressed on my belly to release my own stubborn placenta. When I think about Mary Wollstonecraft, it's hard not to remember that, had I lived back then, I would be dead, too.

But take me out of it. This month, an international group of researchers convened a symposium to discuss the afterlives of *Frankenstein*, especially as the narrative pertains to contemporary discourses surrounding bioethics. For this and related purposes, the researchers were awarded funding from the National Science Foundation. So if we are able to agree that one must understand *Frankenstein* in relation to Mary Shelley's experiences of birth and maternal and infant death, then we must allow the following: that much of literary and cultural history depends upon Mary Wollstonecraft's placenta.

This is not to say that I have boarded the placenta train currently chugging through the bohemianeoliberal enclave where I spent my pregnancy and where I am currently raising my child. No matter what anybody said, I refused to consume my own placenta, to encapsulate it in pill form, to plant it in the backyard. It's not that I was grossed out but that I didn't like the idea of what was once inside going back inside. It is post-feminist to eat the placenta; I want to think the placenta, instead.

I told Nan Z. Da that writing about *Mathilda* had led me to a discussion of the placenta. She said *yes*, and called the eating of the placenta *as circular and glassine as father-daughter incest*.

In *Frankenstein*, *Mathilda*, and *Maria*, we experience problems of release and replacement. There's a sort of scarcity musical chairs, as far as the female characters are concerned. In *Frankenstein*, for example, the scientist's father marries his friend's daughter, thus becoming both "a husband and a parent."[15] Victor's parents adopt their niece, Elizabeth, and determine that she will be Victor's wife. When Victor's mother dies, she tells them, "my firmest hopes of future happiness were placed on the prospect of your union . . . Elizabeth, my love, you must supply my place to your younger cousins."[16] In this way, she ushers in her own replacement—Elizabeth was niece, ward, daughter, sister, cousin, and bride, and now she will be the mother, as well. There's a similar scarcity mindset in *Maria*. Jemima, "famishing (wonder not that I became a wolf!)," advises a man to turn a girl "out of doors" so that he can take her home.[17] This girl, pregnant with the man's child, drowns herself in a watering trough, and Jemima laments, "I thought of my own state, and wondered how I could be such a monster!"[18] In class, students called this scene a simultaneous suicide, abortion, and baptism, a rejection of conditions in which to become a mother would constitute madness.[19] This is just one example of female monstrosity in

Maria, women pitted against one another by a cruel world, the bounds and shackles of the gothic novel no longer an indication of future wealth and happiness but now only a reification of systemic misogyny.[20] I have not yet determined whether Jemima's abortion—which she resists at first, and finally deems necessary—is unique among eighteenth-century novels.

At the beginning of chapter seven, Maria speaks, framing her narrative for the daughter who is missing. Accidentally postmodern, these pages may have, must have called out to Mary Shelley across years and space and lives:

> ADDRESSING these memoirs to you, my child, uncertain whether I shall ever have an opportunity of instructing you, many observations will probably flow from my heart, which only a mother—a mother schooled in misery, could make . . . Death may snatch me from you, before you can weigh my advice, or enter into my reasoning: I would then, with fond anxiety, lead you very early in life to form your grand principle of action . . . Gain experience—ah! gain it—while experience is worth having, and acquire sufficient fortitude to pursue your own happiness; it includes your utility, by a direct path.[21]

My students wanted to talk about Mary Wollstonecraft's struggles with depression, her suicide attempts in the wake of a failing relationship with the father of her eldest daughter. But can we find a place in the cracks between these novels to talk about the radicalism of happiness?

Do you see how I've avoided talking about *Mathilda*?

On the level of the frame narrative, Mathilda's memoirs are penned for her friend, Woodville. She writes, "I do not know that any will peruse these pages except you, my friend, who will receive them at my death." So that she can "dwell upon our friendship in a way that would be needless if you alone read what I shall write," Mathilda has decided to pen her memoirs "as if I wrote for strangers."[22] On the surface, it's a clumsy plot device—a way to have the frame narrative but still tell the story. But if we look closer, we see that Mathilda locates Woodville, her intended audience, as the intimate stranger.

Can I ask you to forget that Woodville supposedly represents Percy Shelley, that the novel was intended for Godwin?

Addressing these memoirs to you, my child, uncertain whether I shall ever have an opportunity of instructing you, many observations will probably flow from my heart, which only a mother—a mother schooled in misery, could make.

He is my only one and although he is so healthy and promising that for the life of me I cannot fear yet it is a bitter thought that all should be risked on one.

Indeed I dare not die. I have a mother whose support and hope I am.

Perhaps the novella is an act of superstitious protection, something like the way my husband and I kept our child's name a secret all through the pregnancy and up until the eighth day after his birth, or the way my sister-in-law would spit when anyone mentioned the baby as she rested, rounded, in her abdomen.

Perhaps it's maternal erasure as maternal sacrifice, as easy as faking your death. Lines from Jack Spicer: "Never looking him in the eye once. All mythology / Is contained in this passage. Never to look him in the eye once."[23] The family romance excludes you to save you. Indeed you dare not die. You have a mother whose support and hope you are.

How could *Mathilda* be for anyone but Percy Florence? Even if he never read it . . . I'm pretty sure he didn't.

4

✦

Clarity

how must that heart be moulded which would not be broken
by what I have suffered . . .
—Mary Shelley, letter to Marianne Hunt, June 29, 1819

Yesterday, the sky opened up during our walk, so we ducked into the hipster breakfast place instead. I was carrying neither a dry change of clothes nor a fresh diaper, and so I felt like a terrible mother, even though I probably looked like a good one, bending in front of the booster seat to retrieve a fallen monkey and being met with a piercing, open-mouth kiss, its two sharp teeth.

This particular breakfast spot is the kind of space people enter in order to feel a certain way. There was a woman eating a cinnamon roll and charcoal-sketching the other customers. There was another woman, young and thin, writing in a romper. A *romper*. And then there was the woman who stood up to speak to me. She was out to breakfast with her eighteen-year-old son, but wanted to tell me that my son looked just like her twenty-one-year-old son, when he was a baby.

He even had an ear like that, she said, pointing at my son's left ear, which flaps down a little bit. He was probably born this way but I once blamed my husband for causing the asymmetry by kissing him too hard. This is one of many things I thought about when a man came up to our table outside the pizza place last weekend, ranting about unequal opportunity. *Not everyone had parents*, he said, *good teachers*. All I could say was *we agree with you, we agree with you, this is true*, and listen, but of course that wasn't enough, wasn't anything, did nothing.

We called it his bendy ear! she continued. *People asked if we were going to give him plastic surgery. Of course we didn't! He grew out of it.* I don't know who this woman hangs around with, who would recommend giving a baby cosmetic ear surgery.

But his name was Vincent, she added, happy, caffeinated, rambling, and I wondered for a moment at the past tense, wondered if her son had died, but the tense corrected itself, and she showed me a picture of a recent camping trip, and she wasn't wistful at all. He just lived in the city, or something.

So the implication here is that the baby—his bendy ear, his unchanged name—somehow existed in the past tense, occupied a separate existence from her *twenty-one-year-old son,* as she called him repeatedly.

We have been traveling frequently, and I've been paying close attention to the speed with which my son can forget people he loves, and then remember them completely. And I've been thinking about how our lives now are something he'll eventually forget. It is not lost on me that I live in somebody else's *when I was little.*

Everything William Shelley lived was a thing he would eventually have forgotten, had he lived. Everything Clara lived, everything Clara Everina lived. Does this mean that their losses were inevitable, at least on some level?

Muriel Spark imagines each scene of trauma with precision:

> Mary's baby was born, a seven-month girl, on 22nd February . . . on 2nd March, the family moved to new lodging, with disastrous results to the delicate premature child, who died four days later.[1]
> . . . after four days' hot, tedious travel [to Byron's villa at Este] Mary arrived with her two children. The baby girl's [Clara Everina's] teething ailment had developed on the journey into a serious illness, and little more than a fortnight later the Shelleys were forced to take her to Venice for medical attention. The child was ill all the way there, and Mary took her straight to an inn while Shelley hastened to fetch a doctor. He was unsuccessful; but meantime Mary had procured a medical man. It was too late; that evening of 24th September [1818], their baby girl died . . .[2]
> But the early heat of Rome rapidly affected three-year-old William, who became ill towards the end of May [1819] . . . Before they

could leave Rome, William's health grew worse. He had fallen victim
of malaria. Fears for him haunted Mary for a week before they were
rapidly confirmed . . . William died on 7th June 1819, and was buried
in the Protestant Cemetery at Rome.[3]

I should mention that Mary Shelley's fifth and final pregnancy would
result in a miscarriage so bloody, it almost killed her.

Daisy Hay comes down a little harder on P. B. Shelley (cf. Anahid's
text about the "trail of tears/dead children"). Hay writes that Shelley
"instructed Mary to pack up and bring the children to Este immediately"
and "enclosed detailed and demanding instructions for the journey."
According to Hay, "it was not a good moment for her to be making an
arduous journey, and Shelley had given little thought to the impact it
would have on both her and their children, William and Clara. His care-
lessness would have disastrous consequences."[4]

I stood up from writing this and attacked my son with kisses. He wasn't
feeling it. *He's in a thoughtful mood*, my husband explained. *Contempla-
tive*, I replied. The baby crawled away, very, very focused on a little plastic
toy, the letter H.

There are a great many biographies of Mary Shelley; consequently, one
can find a great many versions of these events. You can read about Clara
Everina dying in Mary's arms. You can read indictments of William Godwin, who came down hard on his daughter for her grief. But biography is
not my aim, here; biographical reading is not even quite my aim.

It's the freshest part of morning, what my son's favorite book calls "the
hippo break of day," the second day of autumn.[5] Through the teahouse
window, the first yellow leaves of the season are aglow, the top of the
mountain just out of shadow. A man rushes through the room stanch-
ing a nosebleed with his thumb. It's aesthetic, this scene of writing,
something I couldn't imagine I'd ever achieve ten months ago, raw and
bloody and conjoined to my son, who continued to devour my body.
Winnicott says something about the mother seeming unconcerned that
the child wants to eat her.[6] I'm trying to find the exact quote, I'm scroll-
ing through Evan Kindley's Twitter feed, because, I'm telling you, a lot
of very literary people have been discussing Winnicott on Twitter lately.
My mother, psychoanalytically trained, has been saying for years that
Freud will have a comeback; my husband, a cultural anthropologist,

continues, vehemently, to disagree. But I suspect that we lost something when we wrote off the sweatiest offshoot of psychoanalytic literary critique, reader response criticism, which we did even before Stanley Fish moved to Florida and started wearing tracksuits and gold chains and writing about how English professors should stay in their fishbowls. In the summer of 2009, when I was studying at the School of Criticism and Theory and trying to swim off the weight I'd gained visiting ancient French cousins who eat a literal block of cheese every night over conversation—they don't have internet, it's so much better—Stanley Fish gave a lecture on the boundaries of literary inquiry, arguing that political activism of any form was beyond the job description for English professors. The next day, he and I disagreed about whether I could call myself religious. My goldfish, the kind of stupid, sentimental gift one receives when one is newly married, died—yes, his name was Stanley Fish—he ate Gefilte.

This is all to say that I am privileged at a level that makes me uncomfortable, I am cozily ensconced while the world burns, and I am trying to tell you about three babies who died two hundred years ago.

I write this on the 198th anniversary of Clara Everina Shelley's death. Approximately eleven days before Clara Everina died, Mary Shelley wrote to Maria Gisborne, "I hasten to write to you to say that we have arrived safe and yet I can hardly call it safe since the fatigue has given my poor <u>Ca</u> an attack of dysentery and although she is now some what recovered from that disorder she is still in a frightful state of weakness and fever as {*and*} is reduced to be so thin in this short time that you would hardly know her again—."[7] On November 2, she wrote again: "Several events have occurred to us since then, and the principal one, the death of my little Clara—I wrote to tell you of her illness, and the dreadful state of weakness that succeeded to it—In this state she began to cut all her teeth at once—pined a few weeks, and died—."[8]

On September 14, Mary Shelley wrote in her journal, "poor Clara is dangerously ill."[9] On the 24th, she wrote, "This is the Journal book of misfortunes . . . we go to Venise with my poor Clara who dies the moment we get there."[10]

"This is the Journal book of misfortunes." There is something so telling about the overstatement of that phrase, *journal book*, in contrast to the understatement of grief, the "principal event" among "several."

I don't want to psychoanalyze Mary Shelley, but I do want to point out something that's missing. We're looking at Hokusai's *The Great Wave off Kanagawa* but the wave is invisible, we only see the little mountain, and now we're trying to decide where to place a monster in the scene.

Eve Kosofsky Sedgwick writes, "Obsessions are the most durable form of intellectual capital."[11]

Mary Shelley's depression following the death of William is the stuff of legend. Her father made things harder for her but this isn't about him.[12] Two days before William's death, in a postscript to Maria Gisborne, Mary Shelley wrote, "William is in the greatest danger—We do not quite despair yet we have the least possible reason to hope—Yesterday he was in the convulsions of death and he was saved from them—Yet we dare not must not hope . . . The misery of these hours is beyond calculation—The hopes of my life are bound up in him—."[13]

In her next letter, dated June 27, she tells Amelia Curran, "I am going to write another stupid letter to you—yet what can I do—I no sooner take up my pen than my thoughts run away with me—& I cannot guide it except about <u>one</u> subject & that I must avoid—So I entreat you to join this to your many other kindnesses & to excuse me—."[14] Echoes, here, of the creature's survival instinct: "Life, although it may only be an accumulation of anguish, is dear to me, and I will defend it."[15]

Mary Shelley's letters from this period are an accumulation of anguish. She writes: "I never know one moments ease from the wretchedness & despair that possesses me"; "if I would write any thi[ng] else about [my] self it would only be a list of hours spent [in] tears & grief"; "I never am in good spirits—often in very bad—and Hunt's portrait has already seen me shed so many tears that if it had his heart as well as his eyes he would weep too to in pity—."[16]

If art had a heart, it would weep to see Mary Shelley, childless, pregnant, writing *Mathilda*. The mother is a harvester of hearts, pulling new lives from her own body, pulling out her own heart and handing it over and hoping it doesn't get lost, or buried, or eaten, or left in the mud on a rainy walk like that bean-stuffed frog toy of yours that haunts my dreams. Forget that old yarn about Mary Shelley treasuring her husband's heart (more likely his liver) following the poet's cremation.[17] Forget I even brought it up.

When Chet Lisiecki and I were both eighteen, before I became a Romanticist and he became a modernist, when youth held us both, firmly, in the present, we went to hear Rufus Wainwright sing in a small, now defunct venue called 32 Bleu. We were in Colorado Springs, which is very conservative, and for the evening that small space became warm, and queer, and generative. The boys we were dating didn't come with us for one reason and another, and I was secretly glad; I took the new album out from the public library so I could listen before the concert. At one point, Rufus made a comment about the altitude and said he was going to need to "breathe someone else's air tonight," and several men raised their hands; at another point, he dedicated a song to Martha Stewart. All of this is probably dating me, and is to say that I remember that concert less like a concert and more like a conversation among dear friends. As I began to revisit Mary Shelley and motherhood, the song "Harvester of Hearts" started to play and then replay in my head, I mean the version I heard that night, the theme of romantic seduction replaced by maternal longing the way I now hear the word "baby" in pop songs as referring to a literal baby. If you harvest hearts from your own body then you completely vacate yourself. Contrary to modernist manifestos, this erasure occurs at the level of sentiment, or at least passion.[18]

In the back of the reading room, I stand before Amelia Curran's portrait of William Shelley. It dates from Rome, from 1819, and, while I have my suspicions, I refuse to know whether it was painted before or after the child's death. It's an eerie painting—the rose he holds, the rosebud mouth, the green orb of light around his face, the darkness around him—you might even say creepy, though he's not creepy—the child in the painting, I mean. Referring to sleep training, which I refuse to do, a Victorianist texts me: *those bright eyes in the dark.*

5

Elective Affinities

I am always not reading Johann Wolfgang von Goethe's *Die Wahlver-wandtschaften*, often translated as *Elective Affinities*.

Rebecca Ariel Porte says this is because the novel is too formally perfect and so sets off, in me, the impulse to warp.

Goethe incorporated the term from chemistry, indicating the tendency of some substances to combine with others. He applies the concept, instead, to romantic relationships, lowercase and uppercase R.

The novel being, as it is, formally perfect, the characters discuss this concept in chapter four:

> 'Sometimes [things] will meet as friends and old acquaintances who hasten together and unite without changing one another in any way, as wine mixes with water. On the other hand, there are others who will remain obdurate strangers to one another and refuse to unite in any way even through mechanical mixing and grinding, as oil and water shaken together will a moment later separate again.'
> 'It needs little imagination,' said Charlotte, 'to see in these elementary forms people one has known; what they especially suggest is the social circles in which we live.'[1]

The characters go on to explicate the metaphor:

> "Now then!" Eduard interposed: "until we see all this with our own eyes, let us look on this formula as a metaphor from which we may extract a lesson we can apply immediately to ourselves."[2]

Last night, a windstorm swept across the old winter wheat fields around the Denver airport. Our plane landed roughly, jostling against the tarmac, then spun back into the sky like a stone bouncing off the earth.

Like a stone. Why can't I escape this simile? My slow, geologic thinking.

I pressed my lips into your forehead, powerless to protect you. Instead, I tried a meditation technique I learned during pregnancy. With each inhale, I tried to take up all the fear, pain, and discomfort from you. I pictured it as white smoke. On every exhale, I bathed you in the crystalline light of comfort.

We circled for hours, the wind rocking us at odd angles, before we flew to Colorado Springs, landed, refueled, and tried again.

I read you the same book thirty times, to distract you. The book is called *the MONSTER at the end of this book.*

In *the MONSTER at the end of this book*, "lovable, furry old Grover" warns you against the perils of reading. He erects a web of rope, nails the pages together, and lays a brick wall, all in an effort to keep you from turning pages. But, much like Victor Frankenstein, you're driven to create the monster via minute acts of knowledge acquisition. The act of reading—of turning pages—is refigured as an antiheroic feat of strength. (Buried in his crumbled wall, Grover asks, "Do you know that you are very strong?") Grover reframes reading, and knowledge, as illicit, delicious. When I read the story to you, you emit the excited scream you usually save for whole, frozen fish at the grocery store, their glassy eyes.[3]

If the book has a moral, it's the same moral we find in *Frankenstein*: the monster here is you.

In her copy of *Frankenstein*, Muriel Spark wrote, "If there is a moral it is that the creator should [ensure/make?] the creature's happiness if he expects virtue. This applies to all social states."[4]

I can't quite make out the word "ensure" and I think this says a lot about the problems with that moral. Of course happiness helps. But how can we ensure our children's basic safety, let alone their happiness?

This is the question that leaves me quaking long after my feet are back on the ground.

We spend the afternoon asleep together, our bodies a semicolon. I'm aware of how large I look next to you, a lion, a bear. You'll wake up for a few moments, touch my mouth, and fall back asleep.

If literary studies is in the business of knowledge acquisition (*Do you know that you are very strong?*), then why has nobody written a theoretical tractate on elective affinities, on what it means to "work" on something, at least on some level, because we *like* it, by which I mean, combine with it, whether we mean to or not?

The term made its way into the foundations of the social sciences. According to Richard Herbert Howe, Max Weber's "diverse," "informal" use of the term is an "enigma" that, nonetheless, reveals something profound about Weber's thinking.[5] Howe writes, "In the light of the virtual—the order of the possible—elective affinity stands out as a source through which the order of Weber's discourse becomes just visible within his own work as the latent structure of his thought."[6] Howe concludes, "The actors' choices of possible actions are given by the elective affinities of their universe of meanings"; this "order in the universe of possible actions" "makes [Weber's] social science possible."[7]

So what happens if we think this through to our own affinities as literary scholars? Does each literary scholar select from the same "choices of possible actions," or are we strange, thinking substances predisposed to certain combinations? If so, what determines those combinations, and (how) do those determinations change over time?

Complicating readings of Walter Benjamin's seminal essay on the novel, N. K. Leacock argues that "the often-quoted claim that '[t]he mythic is the real material content of this book; its content appears as a mythic shadowplay staged in the costumes of the Age of Goethe' . . . does not in fact summarize Benjamin's reading" because "the mythical element in *Die Wahlverwandtschaften* is reflected, made legible, by an opposing ethical element . . . [that of] character."[8] Leacock explicates Benjamin's understanding of "character by reference to decision" via Aristotle, and goes on to conclude that Benjamin's essay "deserves attention not only from those interested in its development of critical concepts from the dissertation, but also from those whose primary interest is their own relation to a novel like *Die Wahlverwandtschaften*. It is paradoxically this novel's most baffling feature, its overt symmetry or beauty, that provokes readers to move past a superficial response to its figures . . . With any novel, Benjamin's essay suggests, the challenge for the critic is to prolong questioning and postpone judgment, for the problem of character is richer and more difficult than we are always willing to see."[9]

When we were disagreeing about the lyrical ballad "The Last of the Flock," William Galperin leaned in and said, *far be it for me to deny anyone* their *Wordsworth*. I feel the same way about Benjamin, and want to think with Leacock's Benjamin for a second. Here, *Elective Affinities*/elective affinities ask(s) us to "prolong questioning and postpone judgment" as we try to uncover "[our] own relation to a novel." Thus, the long-term relationships we form with literary texts and literary figures are always already a process of self-discovery.

In the 1987 preface to *Mary Shelley*, a revision of her 1951 *Child of Light: A Reassessment of Mary Shelley*, Muriel Spark writes:

> Since the years when I wrote *Child of Light* a great deal has happened to the Mary Shelley scholarship on which this book leans, and a great deal has happened to me. Thirty-six or more years ago the last thing I would have thought of was that I should write a novel, and now I do practically nothing else but write novels.
>   In the introduction to my 1951 edition I wrote: "It is more than time Mary Shelley was reconsidered, especially in her remarkably neglected capacity as a novelist." She is no longer remarkably neglected. *Frankenstein* is widely read, discussed, filmed and televised.[10]

The novelist Jenny McPhee leans in on this elective affinity in an essay titled "Dopplegängers" [*sic*]:

> Mary Shelley died on February 1, 1851. On February 1, 1918, Muriel Spark was born. The two writers shared the same initials. Their last names, under which they wrote, were assumed from husbands. Both wound up single mothers of an only son and both suffered chronic financial worries. These coincidences, for someone with Muriel Spark's mystical temperament, were definitive . . . within the biography's pages Spark is busily and efficiently creating, Frankenstein-like, an identity for herself as a novelist.[11]

I don't buy this, but I like it!

In *Mary Shelley*, Muriel Spark addresses the scene in which the creature first becomes a murderer, strangling Frankenstein's young brother, William, a golden child. Spark writes:

> Richard Church recognised a parallel in Mary Shelley's life when he discussed the murder of Frankenstein's brother, William. "At the time that she was writing this book," Mr. Church remarks, "the baby William was in the tenderest and most intimate stage of dependent infancy . . . It is almost inconceivable that Mary could allow herself to introduce a baby boy into her book; deliberately call him William, describe him in terms identical with those in which she portrays her own child in one of her letters—and then let Frankenstein's monster waylay this innocent in a woodland dell and murder him by strangling."
>
>   It *is* almost inconceivable; and Mr. Church described Mary's motives as a "miserable delight in self-torture." But another suggestion by Mr. Church might give a clue to this coincidence. The creature who murdered William "was a symbol of Mary's overtrained intellectual conscience." The conflict between the emotional and the intellectual Frankenstein was Mary Shelley's also. Her baby, William, we know was the child Mary loved more than any; and when she began to feel her intellect grow under her new task, she automatically identified the child with her threatened emotions.[12]

The dynamic Spark sets up here is one of book vs. baby, the favorite child (I would dispute this claim) a symbol of the emotional life that intellectual work has the potential to obliterate.[13] In the essay "Mother, Writer, Monster, Maid," novelist Rufi Thorpe thinks through novelist Jenny Offill's narrator's conceptualization of the "art monster" and writes that, for Thorpe, the book/baby conflict lies, not between "the mundane and the celestial" but, rather, between "the selfishness of the artist and the selflessness of a mother."[14]

In her copy of *Frankenstein*, at the top of the page on which the creature murders little William, Muriel Spark scrawled, "i.e. emotion [Is/Or/In] Mary's <u>child</u> murdered by her intellect?" Below, a squiggled line highlights the words, "I discovered my lovely boy, whom the night before I had seen blooming and active in health, stretched on the grass livid and motionless: the print of the murderer's finger was on his neck." Read against Spark's marginalia, "print" denotes literary output and circulation, spilled ink and pressed ink obliterating the object of maternal affection.

Image of handwritten marginalia from Muriel Spark's copy of Mary Shelley's *Frankenstein*, The Carl H. Pforzheimer Collection of Shelley and His Circle, The New York Public Library, Astor, Lenox and Tilden Foundations. Reprinted by permission of Georges Borchardt, Inc., on behalf of the Estate of Muriel Spark.

This is some super-problematic, mommy-wars-level exegesis, right here! But it underscores, I think, the connection between anxiety and affinity. And of course the book is crucial, feminist reappraisals of Mary Shelley's corpus having saved her from obscurity.

In *Little Labors*, Rivka Galchen includes a list of writers and details in order to illustrate some trends regarding the book/baby conflict (e.g., "Alice Munro: Three children. Two husbands. First story collection at age thirty-seven."[15]). This is her entry for Muriel Spark:

> Muriel Spark: One child, born in Southern Rhodesia during her marriage to Sydney Oswald Spark, who suffered from manic depression. She moved to London alone, leaving behind her husband. Her young son, also left behind, ended up in the care of some fruit sellers down the

road, before he eventually moved to Scotland to live with his maternal grandparents. The child was later disinherited by his mother, who was annoyed, it is said, that he went around complaining that his mother wouldn't admit that she was Jewish. Among other things. Many books.[16]

Muriel Spark shared a house in the Tuscan countryside with her friend and amanuensis, Penelope Jardine, for more than thirty years. Their platonic life partnership would make an exceptional chick-lit novel, and led Spark to name Jardine as her heir. When "lurid reports [surfaced] of a letter she [Spark] had left explicitly barring [her son] Robin from any claim on her estate," "Robin, an artist, responded by saying he didn't want an inheritance anyway: 'You only need one bed to sleep in, one house to live in. I'm lucky. I've never put great value on money per se.'" Interviewed in *The Guardian*, Jardine said there is a book to be written about famous women falling out with their sons.[17]

On the occasion of the wedding of her only surviving child, Percy Florence Shelley, Mary Shelley wrote a brief note:

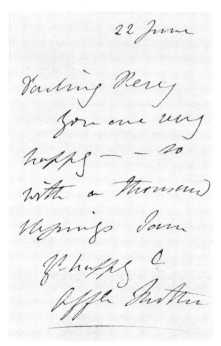

Letter from Mary Wollstonecraft Shelley to Percy Florence Shelley dated June 22, 1848, The Carl H. Pforzheimer Collection of Shelley and his Circle, The New York Public Library, Astor, Lenox and Tilden Foundations.

"You are very happy—so with a thousand blessings I am yr happy & affec[tionate] mother." Notice how "I" and "am" become one word, the pen barely lifted. You are happy so I am happy, I bleeding into am, Mary Shelley pressed into being. You are . . . so . . . I am, iamb, ink blot, heart-beat, this Keatsian math, beauty is truth truth beauty, not because you don't see the monsters, not because you didn't make the monsters, not because you aren't a monster, but because your son is, and so you are.

6

Self

Still I find it hard to get an answer
from the harvester of hearts
— Rufus Wainwright, "Harvester of Hearts"

Capturing something about *Frankenstein* as well as something about pre-natal anxiety, the British psychoanalyst D. W. Winnicott writes that "a mother should want to get to know her baby right away after the birth" in part "because she has had all sorts of ideas of giving birth to some-thing awful, something certainly not so perfect as a baby." He goes on to explain that "it is as if human beings find it very difficult to believe that they are good enough to create within themselves something that is quite good."[1]

I recently had a mid-meeting debate with a colleague about the ethics of auto-ethnography. While postcolonialist in its genesis, my colleague explained that auto-ethnography poses a considerable problem for native studies insofar as it privileges the singular, western subjective perspective. Based on this dynamic, he suggested that all writing in the auto-ethnographic mode is problematic, that is, complicit in oppression.

In *The Vulnerable Observer*, quoting from a panel response she "stayed up almost the entire night worrying and writing, rewriting and worrying, a woman in a hotel room in Texas, listening to the graceful waltz of my husband and son breathing in their sleep," Ruth Behar suggests:

> In my view, it isn't an accident that the effort to engage with the emo-tions in current anthropological and feminist writing follows upon

Freudianisms, structuralisms, and poststructuralisms. I think what we are seeing are efforts to map an intermediate space we can't quite define yet, a borderland between passion and intellect, analysis and subjectivity, ethnography and autobiography, art and life . . . The anxiety around such work is that it will prove to be beyond criticism, that it will be undiscussable. But the real problem is that we need other forms of criticism, which are rigorous yet not disinterested; forms of criticism which are not immune to catharsis; forms of criticism which can respond vulnerably, in ways we must begin to try to imagine.[2]

Yesterday the mom guilt ripped deep as I drove to the airport. My husband's work is in St. Louis this year, so the baby and I flew cross-country to make it to my faculty meeting, the one at which I had the disagreement.

As we were leaving for the airport, the baby squeezed my husband's shoulders and said "da-da." It did not feel great.

The woman in line in front of me at security was traveling without her child. I know she has a child because the security guard tested her bags of pumped breast milk for any signs of explosive contamination. I had to wait so they could check my bottles (of formula, just so you know). She looked humiliated; it was terrible to watch.

Auto-ethnography, I told my colleague, is always about pushback—in this case, by which I mean my case, it's about pushing back against the dominant intellectual modes necessitated and undermined by continental philosophy and by literary criticism after high theory. These modes are productive but they produce via intervention. And when argument is the best way, literature that lends itself to argument becomes the best literature.

Sometimes breast milk shows up as dangerous on the testing strip, the TSA agent told me. *Something about it—something that's in it—I don't know why.*

The question, then, is not whether my interest in Mary Shelley is auto-ethnographic but whether all interest in Mary Shelley is auto-ethnographic.

At a recent conference, I was chatting about motherhood with a circle of women that included Maureen McLane. As so often happens to me when

I'm with poets, I made a grand exclamation, something I didn't know I felt so strongly until I declared it. In this case, I said something like, *no wonder so many of the modernists were men! Only a man would think you can't get away from the self! Just have a baby; the self is obliterated!*

After debating the ethics of auto-ethnography, I think I might add, *only a man would think you* can *get away from the self!* The body, I have learned, has a mind of its own.

In *Mz N*, McLane portrays Mary Shelley's life after Percy Shelley's death in blithe terms:

> . . . Mary Shelley wrote
> prodigiously   Pampered
> her insipid surviving son[3]

But I don't know. In "Tradition and the Individual Talent," T. S. Eliot writes, "The progress of an artist is a continual self-sacrifice, a continual extinction of personality."[4] Later, Eliot concedes, "of course, only those who have personality and emotions know what it means to want to escape from these things."[5] I'm newly interested in the contrast Eliot draws between "personality" and "medium," taking medium to mean both the form and matter of the art and the empty artist as an Orphic channel, occult, Spicerean radio, tradition flowing through, or something.[6] (Am I willfully misreading T. S. Eliot or reading through him?)

To whom is New Criticism a love letter? From Cleanth Brooks to Robert Penn Warren, or from W. K. Wimsatt to Monroe Beardsley? From Reuben Brower to the voice, or from I. A. Richards to the mind? The same poets come up again and again—Donne and Frost, Keats and Hardy. In a 1922 "Comment" in *Poetry* magazine, Harriet Monroe writes of P. B. Shelley: "He had no time to wait or think."[7]

Writing in 1973, in response to what he understands to be a New Critical attack on P. B. Shelley, Wilfrid Converse Barton contends, "Above all the New Criticism, insofar as its assault upon Romanticism is concerned, will fail because it is essentially negative in its principles and in its operations. Anything which lives must be positive. That is why Romanticism, whatever its shortcomings, and Shelley, whatever his deficiencies, are both destined to survive this attack."[8] How can one fail to respond to a vision of literary history as battery operated?

In an article on editing letters as a critical act, Betty T. Bennett, the great champion of Mary Shelley's complexity, writes:

> The primary source of the idea that editing is somehow less than criticism or theory was the New Criticism. Its notion of intentional fallacy, by separating the text from biography and history, made the sole relevant critical act a meditation upon the text. But even that meditation depended upon a stable text. An editor who established that text did so on the basis of the principle of recovering an author's intention, historical significance, aesthetics, or on some other principle of what would be "best." Despite New Critical dicta, therefore, the editor as explained by the New Critic also engaged, however camouflaged, in a critical process . . . The concept that "there is nothing outside the text" means that all decisions are critical ones, not that only some kinds of decisions are critical.[9]

Perhaps the question of auto-ethnography, much like the question of editing or the question of pregnancy, pertains to conceptions of inside and outside.

In an interview on "autotheory" and *The Argonauts*, Maggie Nelson writes:

> I don't make a big distinction between writing about "myself" and writing about "larger issues." (Maybe I'm Emersonian in that way, or just feminist.)[10]

In *The Argonauts*, Nelson honors an obsession with D. W. Winnicott. She writes: "One of this book's titles, in an alternate universe: *Why Winnicott Now?*"; "Winnicott is a writer for whom ordinary words are good enough"; "Winnicott is a fairly sanguine soul"; "*What is good is always being destroyed*: one of Winnicott's main axioms."[11]

Riffing on Winnicott, she explains:

> People say women forget about the pain of labor, due to some kind of God-given amnesia that keeps the species reproducing. But that isn't quite right—after all, what does it mean for pain to be "memorable"? You're either in pain or you're not. And it isn't the pain that one forgets. It's the touching death part.

As the baby might say to its mother, we might say to death: *I forget you, but you remember me.*

I wonder if I'll recognize it, when I see it again.[12]

Four, five hours on Pitocin, no painkiller yet, I'm squatting on a stool in the hospital shower, I'm screaming through my teeth. The water is helping but nothing is helping. I turn to my husband and, as calmly as I've ever said anything, I tell him, *I'm an animal.*[13]

His laughter at that moment—and his apologies for that laughter—cement one meaning in my head, the wrong meaning, the meaning that I'm an animal because look at me go, look what I can endure, bring in the drum line, bang the drums, I've got this.

That was the joke but I meant something else too, what Nelson says about birth and death or what my friend, a pediatrician, told me: *it takes work to enter this world and it takes work to leave it.*

In *The Child, the Family, and the Outside World,* Winnicott offers a theory of stealing as reverting to the state in which one was entitled to take anything from one's mother. Like Eliot confessing that "only those who have personality and emotions know what it means to want to escape from these things," Winnicott must admit that "the shock of having one's bicycle stolen is not, however, mitigated by the knowledge that the thief was unconsciously looking for his mother."[14]

When Evan Kindley discussed this passage on the *Los Angeles Review of Books* podcast, the host said that she'd always thought of breastfeeding as sharing, but admitted that, of course, it *is* stealing.[15]

I told my mom Winnicott is having a moment. She said, *right, because nobody's good enough, so they love that it's good enough!* I leave it to you, dear reader, to decide whether and in what ways she was kidding.

I asked Evan Kindley, *why Winnicott, now?* In part I was wondering why I went to Penelope Leach, instead, which seems, at least in some sense, the less intellectual and more pragmatic choice. But I get it. I'm all about maternal attachment as a feminist act. Plus, my pediatrician recommended it.

Kindley mentioned psychoanalytically inclined graduate students at Princeton in the aughts, turned on to Winnicott by Adam Phillips and Alison Bechdel.

In *Your Baby & Child*, Penelope Leach writes, "If your new baby cries and cries whenever he is put in his crib, guilty soul-searching about your 'mishandling' or his temperament will get none of you anywhere. Stop. Listen to him. . . . Where is he happy? Slung on your front? Then put him there. Carrying him may not suit you very well right this minute, but it will suit you far better than that incessant hurting noise . . . If your three-year-old panics when you turn out her bedroom light, stop . . . Put a light on again and let both of you be content."[16]

This is my philosophy and why my child is not sleep-trained and probably why I do not sleep. (At the time of writing, said child is napping on my husband while my husband reads *Capital*.) I got here in part because of my mother and in part because of Wollstonecraft accessed via Mary Shelley. (They are both sleeping, now.) In *Letters Written in Sweden, Norway, and Denmark*, traveling in search of silver lost in an unfaithful lover's business venture, situated squarely in time between her suicide attempts, trailed by her child (Mary Shelley's older half-sister, Fanny) and her child's nurse, Mary Wollstonecraft writes:

> What, I exclaimed, is this active principle which keeps me still awake?—Why fly my thoughts abroad when every thing around me appears at home? My child was sleeping with equal calmness— innocent and sweet as the closing flowers.—Some recollections, attached to the idea of home, mingled with reflections respecting the state of society I had been contemplating that evening, made a tear drop on the rosy cheek I had just kissed; and emotions that trembled on the brink of extacy and agony gave a poignancy to my sensations, which made me feel more alive than usual.[17]

We can connect this passage to debates about vitalism, their flickering influence in *Frankenstein*.[18] (Winnicott writes: "In each baby is a vital spark, and this urge towards life and growth and development is a part of the baby, something the child is born with and which is carried forward in a way that we do not have to understand."[19]) Or we can look at a letter Wollstonecraft wrote to her lover on this same trip, in which she claimed:

I grow more and more attached to my little girl . . . On ship-board, how often as I gazed at the sea, have I longed to bury my troubled bosom in the less troubled deep . . . and nothing but the sight of her—her playful smiles, which seemed to cling and twine round my heart—could have stopped me.[20]

Two years later, pregnant with Mary Shelley and remarking darkly on Godwin's attentions to another woman, Wollstonecraft would write, "My old wounds bleed afresh . . . I could wish my poor Fanny and self asleep at the bottom of the sea."[21] And twenty-one years later, when Mary Shelley was in the midst of writing *Frankenstein*, "poor Fanny" would commit suicide by ingesting a fatal dose of laudanum. This is how feminism is born—just like everything else.

On Winnicott, Barbara Johnson writes:

Much of his writing involves making the right space for itself ("prepare the ground for my own positive contribution")—situating exactly what he is saying between two things he is not saying. This expanded middle is where Winnicott's unparalleled subtlety is located, between two crudenesses.[22]

Cf. Winnicott: "A mother's love is a pretty crude affair."[23] But Johnson's portrayal of Winnicott's method reveals something about my own. In one sense, I'm writing a traditional, book-length study of Mary Shelley as an expression of her value to me, which is, by extension, an expression of my own feminism. But in another sense, I don't think I'm doing this at all.

Regarding a book review I wrote in the early weeks of my son's life, a commitment I would not back out of because the author was a young woman, and this was her first book, and this was a good journal, Sarah Ehlers said, *you need to channel Winnicott and be a good enough mother to your writing.*

My son, breathing on top of my husband. My husband, breathing under my son. Their cacophonous breath.

Mouth

Professor Veeder said you had an oral fixation, the way you chewed your cuticles red, the diamond below your knuckle. Once, at a conference slumber party, you gnawed your skin in a hotel bed piled high with comparatists. I told you, *you are not a baby ocelot*, and you said, *shut up*. I know all your secrets but I will save them for my novel, I will arrange them in a loose disguise.

In the back of my copy of William Veeder's 1986 *Mary Shelley and "Frankenstein": The Fate of Androgyny*, someone has pressed their finger in ink and left a very deliberate fingerprint, the lines so clear they render identification possible. In his index, Veeder or perhaps his indexer writes:

> Mother: and Percy . . . daughters replacing . . . feminist emphasis on . . .
> male desire to get beyond . . . male need to punish . . . as weak . . .[1]

The year we spent at Chicago together, the campus was dusted with a public art project by Helen Mirra called *Instance the determination*. The project involved text painted directly on the walls, text taken from indexes Mirra created based on Jane Addams's 1907 *Newer Ideals of Peace* and John Dewey's 1925 *Experience and Nature*. In a cryptic, twisted stairwell in the bowels of the English department were painted the words, "Generalities, glittering"; some wayward student affixed an envelope of glitter to the dank and shady wall. I'd dip my fingers in it when I passed. This is neither a method nor an apology.

On the male need to punish mothers, Veeder writes:

> Victor [Frankenstein], like [Percy] Shelley, feels himself failed by women on every side. Elizabeth has both killed his mother and presumed to replace her. Caroline has abetted in this displacement by

dying; she has displaced Victor by introducing the interloper Elizabeth (whom he calls his mother's "favourite" at the very moment
Caroline contracts her lethal fever); and she has joined him incestu-
ously to a sister whose role as mother-surrogate means that Caroline
has wed her son to herself. Like Shelley, Victor responds to such
failures of the ideal by assassination. His nightmare kiss dispatches
Elizabeth to Caroline's grave, where both women can be finished off
by the phallic worms. The monster then appears as the alternative,
the male whom Victor-Laon-Shelley prefers to failed females.[2]

Yes, this is awful, and dated, and problematic. But it is also kind of *right*.
(The phallic worms, especially!) On the intimacy and gender fluidity of
pregnancy, Maggie Nelson writes: "But the pregnant body in public is
also obscene. It radiates a kind of smug autoeroticism: an intimate relation is going on—one that is visible to others, but that decisively excludes
them"; "As my body made the male body, I felt the difference between
male and female body melt even further away"; and "Is there something
inherently queer about pregnancy itself, insofar as it profoundly alters
one's 'normal' state, and occasions a radical intimacy with—and radical
alienation from—one's body?"[3]

You were the first to have a child. I was still living in a dormitory when
you had a child. I taped a roadmap to the back of my closet, thought
about where to go next. I sent you tiny sheepskin boots empurpled with
misunderstanding. The first time we attended a baby shower together,
years later, the basket you brought was grotesque—nipple cream, the best
herbs for a sitz bath, the small tendernesses with which we anoint ourselves once we've been ripped and torn. Veeder argues, "Woman means
death to Victor for the same reason that she does to Shelley—because she
represents flesh itself."[4]

Nelson portrays birth as "touching death." I stopped in the hospital park-
ing lot and pulled down my pants; the waters would not stop; it's the
flood and you realize you're neither Noah nor the ark, you are just the
water trying to bear a vessel through you. And then all of a sudden a year
has passed and you're introducing cartoons in moderation despite the
official recommendations because a big tooth is coming in and your pediatrician friend texts to tell you *risk/benefit ratio = favorable*. At the end
of Pamela Erens's *Eleven Hours*, which I have read in one go because you
(you now, not Nan) are exhausted and will only sleep on me, the nurse,
Franckline, comforts Lore, a new mother, unconscious and in recovery

following a traumatic experience of birth. Erens writes, "This is real, Lore thinks. Franckline is in the world: solid, permanent. Lore tosses between the waters and this still bed."[5]

This is all I want to be for you: solid, permanent. On the final page of a small book shaped like a dog, your imaginary puppy tells you, *I will always be happy to see you, and I will protect you.*[6]

Nan, I can tell a few of your secrets, can't I? Your birth, clear across the world, a mountain village, your mother's cesarean section without medication, or on Tylenol, essentially, her four-month deep sleep, a gun she swung at a crow, calling it an *American bald eagle*, your epidurals and popsicles and sitcoms left on, your two beautiful children brought into the world without any space left open for trauma?

Awake now, my son I mean, and mad for some reason, the milky kiss.

Nan, this is so sentimental, you are going to hate it. You are going to tell me, *you can't put that in your book*, but I *can*, because of my methodological intervention.

We included Merril Bainbridge's 1995 hit "Mouth" on a mix you will forget we made for a dinner party you hosted for some comparatists after they requested "authentic Chinese food." You fed us fish balls in fish broth. In "Mouth," Bainbridge disassociates the oral from the object, thereby cleaving the lover from the act of his objectification. As if she has broken his mouth off his face in a mangled early modern poem, Bainbridge sings, *when I kiss your mouth, I want to taste it . . . don't want to waste it.*[7]

I called you to confess that I had weaned him early, eight months, not the recommended twelve, for a host of good reasons, I knew, but still, and you said *no, it's good, I waited too long to wean and now my son has an Oedipal complex.*

At the dinner party, one of the comparatists made some problematic claims about narrative and truth, and you decimated him, intellectually, and you taught me how to decimate people intellectually with sweet words. Your hand shot up as you disagreed with Veeder when you thought he oversimplified, including once at a class meeting held mere hours after your wisdom tooth extraction, you holding an icepack to your bleeding mouth, a balloon tied to your chair. Later, in the café with a mutual friend, we popped the balloon and found a poem inside, something about angels dancing on the head of a pin.

It's Halloween night, the night after a stupid day, someone else's lost toddler found three blocks down and perfectly all right after much panic, a million phone calls. It's Halloween night, historically my favorite night to go to a party. Nine years ago this night, I saw your father for the third time at a quote-unquote Beakes Street party, by which I mean, a party at a house on Beakes Street. He was not the only anthropologist; he was dressed as entropy; I wore drugstore butterfly wings, a yoga skort, heeled boots. Tonight I'm in my childhood bedroom. You can't fall asleep, so I've got you in the baby carrier, and I'm swaying my hips to my optimistic birthing playlist. Maggie Nelson, again: "It isn't *like* a love affair. It *is* a love affair."[8]

One night this room lit up with a grass fire that blazed across the foothills. I'd been to the top of the neighborhood footpath to see it, I was listening to the Lilywhite sessions, everything was aglow. A boy who interested me, an older boy, had recently confessed that he had put a son up for adoption. I can't believe how young he was, looking back. He'd told me he'd held the child, talked with him a while, and let him go. I hadn't read Blake yet and this felt like experience.

Nan, today your daughter didn't want her "Halloween picture" taken and so I am sending you instead this Halloween picture of me, with Lionel Richie and puffed eyes and eleven-month-old.

Like motherhood, friendship isn't *like* a love affair, it *is* a love affair. On Victor Frankenstein's bestie Henry Clerval, Veeder writes, "Henry Clerval, as well as Victor Frankenstein, 'is' Percy Shelley . . . [Mary Shelley] splits Shelley into 'good' and 'bad' characters because . . . she can deal with him, and with herself, by facing at any one time only a part of either."[9] If Henry represents Victor's better half, then it's no wonder Victor seems to be in love with him. After all, it is Henry's death, and not Elizabeth's, that causes Victor to throw himself on the body, to descend into feverish madness.[10]

Veeder doesn't think so.[11] He argues that the creature's murders proceed "in order of increasing importance of the relationships for Victor: a tie with a child, then with a peer, then with the closest male peer, then with the still closer female peer, and finally the ultimate bond with the father. With each increase of intimacy, there is a greater threat to the self-union which promises immortality . . . father is the supreme threat, because solidarity with him is an alternate ideal."[12] When Henry shows up after Victor has created and abandoned the monster, he asks Victor what's up, and Victor replies, "*he* can tell. —Oh, save me! save me!" and falls down in a fit.[13] I can't read this as a confession of love, but I bet Veeder could. And Victor's promise to create a mate for his creature conveniently provides the occasion for a long trip abroad with Henry and the postponement of Victor's marriage to Elizabeth.[14]

Of course, Victor aborts the project. Apparently, "in a rare example of science settling a literary debate, researchers have concluded that Mary Shelly's [*sic*] hero was absolutely right":

> Writing in the journal *BioScience*, researchers at Dartmouth College describe how they put Shelly's theory to the test.
> They developed a mathematical model based on human population densities in 1816 and the knowledge that the competitive advantages of creatures vary in different environments.
> The worst-case scenario for humans, they found, was a growing population of monsters in South America, as it was [a] less populated region with less competition for resources.
> "We calculated that a founding population of two creatures could drive us to extinction in as little as 4,000 years," said Nathaniel Dominy, professor of anthropology and biological sciences.[15]

In their acknowledgments, Dominy and Yeakel cite an assignment from an English course they took together back in the mid-nineties, an undergraduate thought experiment to which they have circled back. They conclude "by suggesting that the central horror and genius of Mary Shelley's novel lie in its early mastery of foundational concepts in ecology and evolution."[16] And yet all of this also says something about the power of the pregnant body—that the specter of childbirth corresponding to a fictional monstress who never existed *even in her fictional universe* would inspire Frankenstein apologists two hundred years after Shelley began the novel's composition.

In an accidental statement on motherhood, speaking of Victor's periods of illness and weakness, Veeder writes that Victor's father and Henry "can nurse Victor but cannot stop him."[17]

We are alone, somehow, in the Komodo dragon exhibit. He takes a drink of water, first with the long, whipping tongue, then with his whole mouth, the muscles moving in waves down his neck. He notices us as a dog might and comes over; I question, for a moment, the efficacy of the Plexiglas. *Dragon,* I tell you, as you point and ask me, *that?*

8

✦

Rest

On this day two hundred years ago—shortly after her half-sister's suicide and not long before the discovery of Percy's wife, Harriet, pregnant and floating in the Serpentine river—Shelley made in her journal a series of doodles[1] that I cannot decipher:

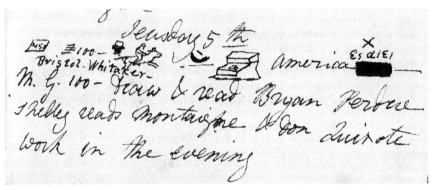

Image of Mary Shelley's journal entry for November 5, 1816, with rebus sketches, MS. Abinger d. 28, fol. 37r. Abinger Collection, Bodleian Library, University of Oxford.

On this day, on Twitter, the "Romanticism blog" (@Wordsworthians) tweets: #OTD 1816 Mary Shelley's journal is full of symbols—a horse-man, a writing desk, a crescent moon. We still don't know what they mean [page/pencil emoji, moon emoji, jockey/racehorse emoji].[2]

Mary Shelley biographer Charlotte Gordon comments, we have some good guesses, though. She's referring to Miranda Seymour's interpretation:

> Mary's journal for the weeks following Fanny's death shows a quiet and intensely studious life, blighted only by money worries and by her increasing impatience with Claire. It is possible that the appearance

of three crescent moon symbols in the journal at this time recorded
disagreements with her stepsister; the moons appear beside references
to the bailiff's visits, however, and these provide an equally plausible
source for coded comment. Shelley, who was fond of Claire, was
reading and writing in the journal; it seems unlikely that Mary would
have made such an overt record of her own hostility when the two of
them were working in close and happy collaboration on her book.[3]

Claire, at this time, had been dumped by Byron and was pregnant with
his child. A moon in my diary means I got my period! On this day, the
seventh day, God, apparently, rested.

Mary Shelley, perhaps writing in 1815,[4] claims:

> All ~~the~~ ideas ~~that these people had formed~~ upon the creation of the
> world & upon ~~all~~ natural phenonoma [*sic*] formed by so illiterate a
> people were of course false . . . God they said had created the world
> in six days—before this time all was void & his spirit floated on the
> face of the waters—he had ordered light to be & there was light—he
> had ordered all animals & all plants to bring forth abundantly after
> their kind & to increase upon the face of the earth—on the sixth day
> he finished his labour & rested on the seventh—.[5]

Shelley goes on to tell the story of the fall and to explain that "Women
were also sentenced to ~~bring forth~~ bear their children with pain to punish
to all posterity the fault of the first mother."[6]

Despite the creation myth being "of course false," my husband is praying,
the baby asleep in a carrier underneath his prayer shawl. And despite this
being the day of rest, I'm at the table behind them, sipping my hot cinnamon coffee and typing, typing furiously.

On the essay quoted above, which she calls Mary Shelley's "first attempt
at political writing," Jane Blumberg writes:

> The Bodleian Library's Abinger deposit c.477 is an extraordinary
> piece of writing by Shelley that has been neither described nor dis-
> cussed . . . It seems to represent a systematic anti-Semitic diatribe in
> that it goes beyond a mere critique of religion to evoke racial ste-
> reotypes current in Shelley's day. Researchers have until now either

ignored the essay, sandwiched as it is between the drafts of *Fran-kenstein*, or found it too crude to examine in detail . . . Shelley's underlying aim was to strike a blow at Christianity by undermining its older foundations.[7]

Blumberg goes on to situate the essay within the matrix of Shelley's early literary and personal influences, ultimately arguing:

> In the context of other such works, we understand that she no doubt intended to extend her condemnation of the Jews to religion in general. As it stands, her argument is clouded because she gives her Biblical Jews contemporary racial stereotypical characteristics and her radicalism is undercut by her failure to establish the despotic tendencies in *any* monotheistic religion. But this failure may anticipate the later Shelley who in complete contrast to her husband found it impossible to condemn Christianity. In fact, she had become a church-goer before PBS's death, and after it took comfort in the promise of life after death as the only means to relieve her suffering.[8]

A file of Betty Bennett's notes and emails reveals her suspicion that Mary Shelley did *not* write this essay but was, instead, "doing a French exercise in translating rather than simply reading the text." In private correspondence, Bennett writes that the "tone & most of the perspective are totally inconsistent with MWS, early & late!" In a document that looks like form copy for emails and letters, Bennett writes, "There is sufficient internal evidence to demonstrate that the draft-essay is one of several exercises in translation, probably from French. In the interest of scholarly accuracy, and clearing Mary Shelley's name of having written so crude and vitriolic an attack on Jewish history, I am trying to locate the exact source of the original and its author."[9]

In addition to Mary Shelley's failure to condemn religion, Blumberg focuses on Shelley's discomfort with "the violence inherent in radicalism" and her sense that evil, in man and in the world, might be "destined to triumph."[10]

On Noah, Shelley writes, "God determined to save him & therefore ordered him to build a clumsy kind of machine called an ark."[11]

An ark is "a clumsy kind of machine" and so is a mother.

On this day last year I was so big I could no longer do prenatal yoga on the mat—I had to lean against the wall in order to move my legs in relation to each other beneath the orb of my belly.

This day last year was exactly one week before my water broke and the deluge moved through me, bearing my son three days later.

There is a conference paper I am always not writing about Romanticism as a form of secular spirituality for postwar American Jews. In a very specific academic fantasy, I deliver this paper at the Association for Jewish Studies annual conference. I'm wearing my great-grandmother's bracelet, as I often do—a thin, silver chain engraved with the words *sei gesund*, good health, be well, get real. My paper, in the fantasy, takes M. H. Abrams's *The Mirror and the Lamp* as its key example, and thinks about young, radical Wordsworth, and labor, and unions, and Yiddish secularist culture, and about the key figures of Romanticist thought in relation to Jewish identity, which lets us think about high theory writ large in relation to Jewish identity and from a neo-Spinozist perspective. This is an achievable fantasy but the paper is too perfect in my head for me to profane it with actual typing.

On Lionel Trilling, Robert Alter writes:

> The undercurrent of insecurity about belonging to the genteel world of Western letters occasionally rises to the surface in certain pieces that painfully reveal the writer's ambivalence toward his Jewishness. One suggestive document of this sort is "A Friend of Byron" (1926), a study by a very young Lionel Trilling of Isaac Nathan, the man who set the *Hebrew Melodies* to music and also wrote critical observations on Byron's verse. The tone of the essay is so self-consciously British and literary, and "poor Nathan," the culturally aspiring Jew, is treated with such appalling condescension, that it is almost as if Trilling, himself the son of an immigrant, had invented a persona through which to speak: we are allowed to see the alien Jew of mediocre talents only from an immense, stultifying distance of erudite, British otherness . . . There is a pleasant and perhaps even instructive irony in the fact that Lionel Trilling, who was to become a very good critic, would one day quote the rabbis effectively to support *his* opinion of Wordsworth's verse. The distance between this early piece and his "Wordsworth and the Rabbis" (1950) can be taken as a partial measure of how much more securely placed the Jewish

writer had become in the Anglo-American intellectual world by the 1950's.[12]

Marjorie Levinson takes up Trilling's phrase, arguing that the lyrical ballad "Michael" must have been conceived by "the 'Jewish Wordsworth,'" a concept that helps us understand how Wordsworth "situate[s] poetry as a primary product capable of performing various offices (viz., persuasion, pleasure) without further conversion, although he consistently recognizes the processed, or value-laden character of all discursive materials."[13]

On Harold Bloom, David Kaufmann writes, "*The Anxiety of Influence* meditates on and is driven by the furious ambivalences of assimilation. Part of its genius lies in its ability to cast the Romantics in the role of Jewish aspirants to culture while hiding the particularly Jewish anxieties that undergird this account of Romantic aspiration. Is this merely an example of Bloom's ability to project his own situation onto the Romantics, a remarkable act of *chutzpah* on his part? Or does this tell us something about the Romantics? . . . we can ask if Bloom's theory does not also provide a trenchant analysis of the 'Romantic Ideology' by showing us the social anxieties that sustain it."[14]

Kaufmann goes on to implicate Levinson in his analysis, though I'm not sure I agree with his interpretation of her. In any case, the notion of critical *chutzpah* he develops pertains, I think, to the question of elective affinities. Foregrounding one's elective affinity as a critic is "a remarkable act of *chutzpah*," but that doesn't mean the affinity isn't there if one lacks *chutzpah*, that is, if one fails or refuses to acknowledge one's "own situation."

Marjorie Levinson has long been my spirit guide through the Romantic period. But does that mean my Jewishness—mediated by or reflected in my early perceptions of her Jewishness, which I formulated as a graduate student without a strong area of specialization—is part of the calling card that led me to my field, the scattershot framework of elective affinities that led me and leads me to experience pregnancy, childbirth, and motherhood in relation to Mary Shelley?

This seems all wrong. I came to graduate school interested in mathematics and modernism, signed up for Marjorie's course because I'd loved reading her in a class on fragments and ruins, realized that modernist engagements with mathematics were neo-Romantic, traced the intellectual history back. My story of how I came to be who I am as a thinker really has nothing to do with the candlesticks my great-grandmother carried across the Atlantic Ocean, my mother's father hiding in a barn at six years old. But I suppose I cannot say for sure.

If I were a person who got tattoos, which I might be, were I not a Jew, and I had to choose from Mary Shelley's hieroglyphs, their alternate alphabet, I'd choose the "crescent moon" which looks, to me, not like a moon on its back but like a belly.

In *Bah! Said the Baby*, a baby says bah, and his family members can't figure out what he's indexing. They bring him a bottle, a bear, a book.[15] We review these signs and symbols often, you trailing your finger across the page, until one day you come to the question mark, asking with your eyes and your insistent hand and your limited words, demanding to know what hovers over the baby's head.

The morning after the election, I get up because I have a young son, and that means I'm in the business of world creation. Worlding, dwelling, whatever Heidegger (a Nazi?) would call it. Despite that sinking feeling, together worlding a world.

9

✦

Identity

We had my husband's colleagues over for dinner and ended up in a discussion of the "girl fight" as an ontological category.

The concept came up because we were discussing a key moment in a recent presidential debate, a moment of particular brilliance on the part of the candidate we all supported, which had to do with making a real girl-fight move, by which I mean, the move to which there is no acceptable counterattack.

As opposed to academic argumentation, which not only presupposes but also anticipates pushback, the art of the girl fight lies in saying the thing to which the only possible response is acquiescence. One can only win the girl fight by refusing to respond.

So, when my friend, upon realizing that her husband is about to forget his mother's birthday, buys a very lovely gift, and wraps it beautifully, and finds the perfect card, and has each grandchild sign it, and her mother-in-law's response upon opening the gift is to say, *it must be nice to have a husband who works so hard so that you can buy extravagant presents*, my friend says nothing. It doesn't feel great, but she has won the girl fight!

Or take Tina Fey's *Mean Girls*, which is essentially girl-fight *Fight Club* and which my students often suggest is a retelling of *Frankenstein*. There's a moment in the movie when queen bee Regina George, asserting her social dominance as exemplified by the possession of a particularly coveted boyfriend, turns from the young man she is grooming to face Cady, her frenemy and our wayward protagonist. In a voice of quiet control, Regina demands, "Cady, will you please tell him his hair looks sexy pushed back?"

In voiceover, Cady tells us she knows how this would be resolved in the animal kingdom, and we get a scene of the girls fighting like lionesses, their fellow high school students whooping and hollering, wild animals in jeans and T-shirts, the claws quite literally coming out.

But this was girl world, voiceover Cady reminds us, even as Cady utters, "Your hair looks sexy pushed back." *And in girl world, all the fighting had to be sneaky.*[1]

Cady has lost the girl battle, but she will win the girl war.

The girl fight is a misogynistic social construction, and quite a brilliant one, at that. From a young age, society trains women to compete with one another in subtle ways that don't undermine their aesthetic appeal or use value. Girl fights are a great distraction from other, more important or subversive things that girls could hypothetically be doing. (Cf. Jemima's story in *The Wrongs of Woman, or Maria*.) But what happens when all that ugliness becomes visible?

In an episode of *New Girl* appropriately titled "Girl Fight," an argument escalates between Jess and Cece as the result of male friends' well-meaning interventions. Ultimately, this culminates in a brawl at a baby shower that only concludes when Jess affixes the suction cups of a breast pump to Cece's eyes, landing them both in the hospital. Similarly, in the *Mean Girls* dénouement, Regina George precipitates her own downfall by publishing the "burn book," a collection of potent rumors. Spewing unverifiable hate may seem like a good distraction from the fact that she's losing her power as a bully, but things don't go so well for her, in the end.

Well, here's the thing about academic intervention.

I am trying to write my way into a discussion of Anne Mellor and Betty T. Bennett, who did not like one another, at least as far as I can tell.

Now, I want to be very clear. I am not accusing Mellor and Bennett of being in a girl fight! Their differing perspectives on the connections between Mary Shelley's personal relationships and her literary output were lucid and argumentative; the debate between them was scholarly and open. It's just that I want to talk about their debate in a kind of girl-fight way, by which I mean, a way that precludes response.

Unlike Betty Bennett, Anne Mellor is alive, and so I was able to talk to her about Mary Shelley and motherhood and elective affinities. I asked her how and whether she might connect her intellectual devotion to Mary Shelley to her own experiences of motherhood. Our conversation led, after a while, to a discussion of Mellor and Bennett's disagreements about Mary Shelley, and the possibility of grounding these disagreements in the scholars' own life experiences. Reflecting on her interpretation of William Godwin in an essay on the problems with life writing, Mellor asks, "Did I respond in this way because my own childhood relationship with my father was extremely conflicted? Because my father clearly preferred my sibling, my younger sister? Because after my father divorced my mother when I was eighteen in order to marry his mistress, he intentionally abandoned his first family and has seen me only three times in the last thirty years? As a close friend and former colleague once said to me, 'A woman who loved and felt close to her father would write a different book on Mary Shelley.' "[2] In our conversation, Mellor suggested that Betty Bennett was just such a "woman." According to Mellor, while she herself had a problematic relationship with her father and a first marriage that ended in divorce, Bennett had a loving relationship with her own father and was widowed at a young age. Mellor suggested that their competing senses of Mary Shelley's biography—their disagreements about how far to take criticisms of Mary Shelley's husband and father, in particular—pertained to their very different *auto*biographies.

I do not want to make an academic argument about this! After all, what would such an argument be—that the feminist scholars responsible for ensuring Mary Shelley's canonicity were, all the while, working out their own relationships with the men in their lives? This is a terrible, problematic, antifeminist argument. It's also not what I believe to be true. And yet, the structures of literary-historical inquiry leave little room for a more nuanced interpretation.

So how about this . . . Betty T. Bennett and Anne Mellor, two intellectual heavyweights, two skilled researchers, two beautiful readers, two staunch feminists, worked tirelessly to ensure that I—who just subscribed to *Teen Vogue* because I think it asks "girls" and by extension everybody to look beyond wealth, power, and flashy distraction machines to systems of injustice and oppression in the tradition of the gothic novel, who stayed up too late last night watching a Japanese reality television show, who sends a self-congratulatory text to a group called "Best Witches" every time I spend an uninterrupted hour writing, who still regrets once telling a college classmate that I wouldn't call myself a feminist because I didn't quite understand what it meant, and who is flawed in a great many other ways—could have Mary Shelley. Could have her when I needed her. And, man, did I need her when I was pregnant. When the blood was rushing from my body after three days of labor and a new nurse came in and said *your mother is here I told her you're still alive.* On election night. And they knew I would need her because they needed her and I don't need to understand why they needed her. But *that* they needed her and that there is no unproblematic way to discuss why or how they needed her tells us that something is wrong with our theory and with our praxis.

What do you have to say to that? See, I told you. *Girl fight.*

In *Mary Shelley: Her Life, Her Fiction, Her Monsters*, Anne Mellor argues that it is out of "the fear of a woman that she may not be able to bear a healthy, normal child and the fear of a putative author that she may not be able to write, that Mary Shelley's nightmarish reverie was born . . . Significantly, Mary Shelley dedicated the novel to Godwin, even though he had disowned her after her elopement, rather than to Percy Shelley who helped her with its composition. She wanted to give the book to its father, *her* father, for the book is her created self as well as her child."[3]

In our conversation, Mellor told me that her son was born after a fifteen-hour labor. The doctor held him up, and Mellor was shocked by his huge, monstrous blue testicles. She said she *flashed on this horrible looking thing.* Her doctor explained that the baby's hormones had been at war with hers, inside her body, that the next day he'd be fine; indeed, he was. But Mellor imagines that Mary Shelley must have had that moment with her son William, a moment of *not immediate overwhelming joy.*

Mellor went on to suggest that *women who have not been mothers lack something in terms of understanding* Mary Shelley's dreams of her dead daughter, the *immediate reaction* to a created being that's *hard* rather than joyous. (Just to be clear: *this* is a girl-fight move.[4])

In our conversation, Mellor clarified that while social, cultural, political, and scientific discourses came to bear once Mary Shelley sat down to write *Frankenstein, we wouldn't have had the book if she hadn't been so multiply pregnant and hadn't had the first baby.*

Let me play girl fight's advocate. (See also: how to lose a girl fight.) In a way, I *didn't* understand *Frankenstein* until I became pregnant; at least, I understand it differently now. (Not to be too formalist, but the news this week reported a scientific study that suggests the actual anatomy of my brain shifted during my pregnancy.[5]) But that's what literary criticism is for, isn't it—for guiding a reader through one's original or, in my case, not quite original interpretation? Is the literary critic a kind of mother or monster, the public embodiment of marginal, delimiting knowledge? To interpret the text is to harvest its heart. But texts don't have hearts. The literary critic asks you to interpret her text with her in her way, which is to say, to harvest her heart. To be the mother so that she can be—so I can be—the monster.

10

✦

Infant Vows

A broken screen at the bus station reads *this is only a test, this is only a test* and I wish it were true.

The night of the election, I begin to recite a myopic koan to myself, *my little boy, my little boy, my little boy.* I do this because my distress—my anger at voter suppression, my fear of bigotry, misogyny, and hate—is keeping my son awake, then waking him from dreams I cannot imagine, because this is not something one can explain to a one-year-old. I don't know what he knows, or thinks, or sees.

To be a mother is to engage in the project of world creation. So even as the world falls apart, I sing a simple song, I help the little zookeeper feed the plastic leaf to the little hippopotamus, I tilt the hippo's chin back to release the prerecorded burp.

On the first pages of *Mathilda*, a young woman, isolated, tells us, "no voice of life reaches me" yet "there is a slight, quick spirit within me."[1] Mathilda herself is not pregnant, is explaining a state of excitement that her death has finally come, but Mary Shelley is pregnant, with Percy Florence. By now she has lost Clara, and Clara Everina, and even William.

The night of the election, my son discovers a book from my own childhood called *Duckling Sees*. It is by someone named Hargrave Hands. On the first page, a duckling, newly hatched, sits atop the eggs of his future siblings, gazing up at a white duck. Hargrave Hands tells us, "Duckling sees who watches over the eggs . . . Her mother."[2] The mother duck's face is serious, mindful, concerned. But perhaps I am projecting.

Mathilda tells us, or really she tells her friend, Woodville, who many read as an emblem of Percy Bysshe Shelley, "I shall relate my tale . . . as if I wrote for strangers."[3] Beginning her tale, she explains, "it is my last task, and I hope I have strength sufficient to fulfil it . . . My fate has been governed by necessity, a hideous necessity."[4] We can misread this, I think, we can misread this and see a mother who has lost three children yet must continue to live for the life inside her, a stranger, out of necessity.

The world is falling apart and so I will allow myself to misread. A student in my department calls this the *fuck-it stage of grief.*

Mathilda begins her tale by introducing us to her father, whom she never names. A spoiled but congenial rich kid, he keeps secret from his bros a deeply felt love for a childhood playmate, Mathilda's future mother, Diana. "He could not bear that they should blaspheme it by considering that trivial and transitory which he felt was the life of his life."[5] You are, quite literally, the life of my life, the life that came from my life, bare and bore and born.

Though she really can trust in her future husband's affections, Diana fears that "other attractions and fickleness might make him break his infant vows."[6]

But she's wrong—the father's love for Diana "was a passion that had grown with his growth; it had become entwined with every faculty and every sentiment and only to be lost with life."[7] I cannot help but picture Mary Shelley's quite literal growth as she wrote *Mathilda*, her skin stretching over the globe. The way our organs rearrange—my stomach growling below my breast, my heart beating under my arm, the taste of acid in my mouth.

"Diana filled up all his heart: he felt as if by his union with her he had received a new and better soul."[8]

But in an oft-remarked parallel to Godwin and Wollstonecraft, this love affair cannot last long: "Fifteen months after their marriage I was born," Mathilda explains, "and my mother died a few days after my birth."[9] What happens to Mathilda, then, is often read biographically. Elizabeth Nitchie, who would later edit *Mathilda* for publication, writes of the then-unpublished work:

> In her fiction she objectified her own traits, creating both morbidly
> reserved and bad-tempered characters. Once at least the two faults

are combined in one person: not even her worst enemy could say harsher things about Mary [Shelley] than Mary says about herself in the obviously autobiographical *Mathilda*. Written at the end of the tragic nine months during which both her children had died, this novelette was the fruit of the deep depression of spirits into which Mary fell. Her black moods had made her difficult to live with . . . Mary well knew what she was doing to [her husband]. In an effort, perhaps, to purge her own emotions and to confess her guilt in the late summer of 1819, she poured out on the pages of *Mathilda* the suffering and the loneliness, the bitterness and the self-recrimination of the past months.[10]

Charlotte Gordon's take inverts this harsh interpretation:

In fictional form, Mary articulated her rage at Shelley's desertion. Instead of supporting her, Shelley had stepped back and was studying her, using her as a model for Beatrice [in *The Cenci*] . . . One can almost picture Mary writing these words in the garden while Shelley was out walking with her stepsister or up on the rooftop in his glass cell.[11]

Nitchie goes on to argue, "Mathilda is certainly Mary herself."[12] She cites a number of parallels:

Like Mathilda's, Mary's mother died a few days after giving her birth. Like Mathilda's, her father had been, though dogmatic and self-centered, "a distinguished member of society; a Patriot; and an enlightened lover of truth and virtue," whom now his friends remembered "as a brilliant vision which would never again return to them." Like Mathilda, she spent part of her childhood in Scotland . . .

And certainly Mathilda is the Mary of that sad year. She is the Mary who wrote to Miss Curran after William's death: "Let us hear also, if you please, anything you may have done about the tomb, near which I shall lie one day, and care not, for my own sake, how soon. I never shall recover that blow; . . . everything on earth has lost its interest to me." Mathilda described herself as "one who had shut herself from the whole world, whose hope was death and who lived only with the departed."[13]

I think Nitchie is missing two things, here. The first is *for my own sake*, the second, *on earth*. Unlike the tomb, the womb is not or is not only an earthly dwelling. In Scotland with her cold aunt and the doting nurse she'll eventually lose (Mary Shelley also had a nurse like this), Mathilda "cannot say with what passion I loved every thing, even the inanimate objects that surrounded me. I believe that I bore an individual attachment to every tree in our park; every animal that inhabited it knew me and I loved them. Their occasional deaths filled my infant heart with anguish."[14] Cf. Jane Bennett, who roots her conceptualization of "vibrant materiality" and her examination of the "material agency or effectivity of nonhuman or not-quite-human things" both in the history of philosophy and in the experiences of childhood, in which, Bennett suggests, the "world [is] populated by animate things rather than passive objects."[15] In William Wordsworth's "We Are Seven," a traveling man insists that a young girl's departed siblings are in heaven, while the girl insists that they are in the ground. Spoiler alert: they are in the ground.[16]

After Diana's death, Mathilda tells us, her father "would never see me" and left in such a way that he "became at once, as it were, extinct." But he leaves one fossil, a letter, in which he implores of his sister, "As for that unhappy little being whom I could not see, and hardly dare mention, I leave her under your protection. Take care of her and cherish her: one day I may claim her at your hands; but futurity is dark, make the present happy to her."[17]

It is not enough—not even close to enough—but one has to start somewhere. *My little boy, my little boy, my little boy.*

Charlotte Gordon points out that Mathilda's statement, at the story's end and at her death—"'*A little patience, and all will be over*'"—"link[s] her to her author and her author's mother," as these "are the deathbed words spoken by Wollstonecraft, Wollstonecraft's mother, and the mother in Wollstonecraft's last novel, *Maria*."[18] But *Mathilda*, read biographically, is the opposite of surrender, a link between the loss of children and the reincarnation of maternal identity.

The opposite of surrender. What I want to find, beyond my worry stone, my little book, my little boy.

Two days after the election, at a committee meeting, my colleague rolled something around in her hand: a rock imprinted with the word *courage*.

Who swims in the pond? Hargrave Hands asks, by way of a conclusion. *Duckling sees her family.*

11

Imagination

In at least two places in her archive, Betty T. Bennett saves Frankenstein's creature. The first of these is an adaptation of *Frankenstein* for the stage. Watch the end.

FRANKENSTEIN

I don't want to die.

MARY SHELLEY

William. Justine. Clerval. Elizabeth.

FRANKENSTEIN

[Frankenstein lays down, covers himself, convulses as Creature did in beginning and dies; arm cast out from sheet, head toward audience]

CREATURE

And me?

MARY SHELLEY

I suppose we might try. [Mary Shelley exits up aisle; Creature follows.][1]

On her many years of editing Mary Shelley as a feminist act, Bennett spins *Tradition and the Individual Talent*: "Evidence, both critical and editorial, demonstrates that feminists can reveal the complex intellect in women's art . . . Particularly in this era of restoring women to their rightful places in literary history, subtle and not so subtle influences on feminists' own lives contend. We all recognize it is impossible to free oneself from such influences; indeed, there are reasonable arguments to suggest critics gain from just such influences."[2]

The second archival instance in which Betty Bennett preserves Frankenstein's creature is in an unfinished document called *The Lost Journal*. The title refers to a journal Bennett describes in her unfinished biography of Mary Shelley:

> The new journal, which runs from 14 May 1814 through 21 July 1816, is a source of particularly fascinating information about MWS. It chronicles the birth of the Shelleys' son William and the beginning of CC's tempestuous affair with Lord Byron. It also describes the first ?month [sic] of the 1816 Geneva summer, when a contest one rainy night between the Shelleys' [sic] and their friends stimulated MWS to write her masterpiece, Frankenstein. But that journal has never been found.[3]

While any reasonable person would have to read Bennett's *The Lost Journal* as an unfinished short story or as the beginning of a novel, I would like to take the title at face value, for a moment, and ask what it would mean for this document to be the lost journal of prominent Mary Shelley scholar Betty T. Bennett.

At one point in *The Lost Journal*, Bennett writes of herself, "But I am a strong woman. Everyone has always said so. Even when she is not sensible, she is strong."[4]

In *The Lost Journal*, "Professor Bennett" is forty years old, bored, dating a man she knows she'll never marry. In the document, which is addressed to her brother in much the way *Mathilda* is addressed to Woodville, she recounts a strange correspondence. A man writing on nineteenth-century stationery and calling himself William Frankenstein reaches out to her. He tells her, "I have always been interested in the peculiar sympathy you seen [sic] to exhibit for your subject and for the topic of the monster."[5] He tempts her with archival fragments and the promise of information. Initially, Professor Bennett is incredulous:

> Surely my correspondent wanted to see just how much a fool I was or perhaps how lonely. I looked in the mirror to see if there were lonely lines around my eyes, or perhaps my mouth had begun to pucker and develop those tense little lines from pouting too much. Or was it my hair? Was my hair turning gray? I looked carefully—one or two gray hairs, but on the whole no—dark brown. Clearly, my William Frankenstein was appealing to features that the eye could not see.[6]

In a moment that feels more confessional than playful, Professor Bennett tells us about the guy she's dating, Howard, tells us how "I often felt like a pine tree whose top had been lopped off. I grew. I still grew. The ends of my branches turned bright green in the May rains. But I was slightly lopsided, leaning out from under the surrounding oak, looking for sun, but already rooted, I could only peer out and find haze. Howard was the haze."[7]

That stupid aphorism: *bloom where you are planted.* Jesus, Howard, if you are or ever were real, I hope you're not reading this.

Professor Bennett breaks it off with Howard, who thinks this must be a prank. She calls her brother and has a conversation with him in her head and doesn't need his advice any more when he calls back: "For years, you had argued that I possessed all the strength and energy that any woman ever did. Stop asking other people for advice, he said. Do what feels right to you. You will be more at home with yourself when you do things without asking for guidance. So I decided that this would be my first great secret."[8]

She writes back, travels to London. Every luxury has been prepared for her, but her correspondent never appears. She returns home, has the sense she's being followed, hears from her mysterious interlocutor, travels to Geneva. I am not making this up. She calls airplanes "time machine[s]" because "they set you down in a different country at an unexpected hour."[9] She rereads *Frankenstein* on the plane and writes, "Thus the time machine carried me comfortably back to the early 19th century."[10] Books, then, are time machines, too.

As in London, her transportation and airfare have all been arranged. After a few days, a car arrives, and carries her, in a black evening gown, up, up Mont Blanc. Her host is still nowhere to be seen; an Elizabeth waits on her; she sets to work transcribing letters of Mary Shelley's, letters that suggest mysterious meetings during the summer of 1816. "The tone of the letters grew more and more familiar, and several were signed Mary, a signature she reserved almost exclusively for Shelley. Who then was this Monsieur with whom Mary Shelley had become so intimately connected in the summer of 1816? She, the beloved mistress of Shelley, or was it possible that Shelley knew of this friendship—that their friends knew of this friendship—that it was only a secret from the future—that the friendship was only accidentally hidden."[11]

Professor Bennett realizes she is a prisoner, realizes her host is Franken-stein's creature, falls ill or maybe mad, recovers, decides she must plan her escape, gets in the practice of hiking. Perhaps she thinks she's in *Dracula*, or something like it; as *Frankenstein* reminds us over and over, you're not always in the story you think you're in. She doesn't want to confront the creature but he corners her during her attempted escape, begins to tell his side of the story. As the story begins, however, the manuscript ends.

What might it mean to take this document seriously, by which I mean, not only to imagine that it might be true, but also, or alternately, to imagine that it might be true even if it's fictional? What might we make of this manuscript, which I found in the way so many Romantic novels claim to be found—lost, left behind, unfinished? What might it mean to think about the "complex intellect" in this manuscript as something that doesn't fit into editorial or critical scholarship, and is it possible that scholarship suffers a deficit when this intellect has to go somewhere else? And what, then, of friendship, of friendship by literary history "accidentally hidden"?

Writing down her life story—for whom, if not for me?—my great-grandmother Clara explained, *Leaving my home town was my first journey alone, it was the beginning of a new life for me . . .* and *My mother felt that I had a good voice, and promised, to have me take lessons to develop it but when the time came for me to start her fear was that I would leave Home—But as you see—you cannot figure out Life, I left Home anyway.* She wrote, *It was different those days. The parents would sit in the parlor and enjoy the art of their children. Believe me it was wholesome and good . . .*

> *One nice day uncle ask me if I would like to go with him to America, just on a visit for one year . . . My first thought was how to leave my mother, with my father and sister gone—*
> *But being a young girl, I received the invitation, with a joy and expectations to be able to see the new world called, America . . .*
> *Mother accepted the news with choking emotions, after composing herself she kissed me and wished me luck, at that moment.*
> *There were thousand and one thing on her mind, one I knew, was her promise to cultivate my voice which she did not, because being afraid me to leave Home—*
> *. . . while my mother took care for the right close [sic] for me, on my trip to wear. The time was passing quick mother never stopped, to teach me how to take care of myself . . .*

As the ship started on the 8 day voyage to U.S.A. the band begin to play, at that moment, I was in tears, in spite of the good people around me, trying to comfort me, just then I realize that I left my home, not for one year, but for the rest of my life.

Regarding her room at the creature's mountain home, in which there did not initially appear to be a mirror, Professor Bennett tells us, "But I was wrong about the mirror. It simply took finding."[12]

12

Lost

On *Mathilda*'s textual history, Graham Allen writes:

> Although written in 1819, *Matilda* was not published until Elizabeth
> Nitchie's edition in 1959. The story behind that one hundred and
> forty year hiatus is an inevitable part of any reader's engagement with
> *Matilda*. The text concerns the incestuous desire of a father for his
> daughter, his suicide after confessing that desire and then the daugh-
> ter's melancholic movement towards a wished-for death. Shelley sent
> *Matilda*, in the care of her friend Maria Gisborne, to her father in
> 1820. Godwin pronounced the story "disgusting and detestable,"
> lamented the lack of "a preface to prepare the minds of the readers,
> and to prevent them from being tormented by the apprehension from
> moment to moment of the fall of the heroine," and seems to have
> refused to return the manuscript to his daughter after deciding not to
> send it to the publishers.[1]

Godwin did not return the text but I wish to return to the text.

On the relationship of our *Mathilda* to this confiscated draft, E. B. Murray writes:

> *Mathilda* was finally edited from a microfilm of the Bodleian holo-
> graph manuscript . . . by Elizabeth Nitchie . . . Mary's insistence that
> Maria Gisborne get the manuscript of the novel from Godwin so that
> a copy might be made suggests that he had a unique holograph.[2]

In other words, while we have a manuscript draft for *Mathilda*, and while
that manuscript shows us how Mary Shelley moved away from a "fanciful setting" that might have connected the story to Wollstonecraft and/or
to Percy Shelley (and/or provided Godwin with the preface he desired),

the "final" copy, that is, the copy Mary Shelley may have intended to publish, is lost.[3] As I write this, a new edition is in production, which Michelle Faubert re-transcribed directly from Shelley's manuscript.[4] In contrast to *Frankenstein*—collaboratively edited, compulsively edited, perhaps, in the end, over-edited—*Mathilda* relies on other hands to bring her into the world.

In her book proposal, Faubert promised that her methodology would constitute an act of fidelity to the text; I might suggest that it also constitutes a feminist act of fidelity to Mary Shelley.

While we discuss the manuscripts and editions we do have, I also want to think about the manuscript we don't have, which occupies a genre similar to what Betty T. Bennett calls "wordless letters."[5]

I do not want to illuminate Godwin as a point of erasure through which Wollstonecraft's placenta and Mary Shelley's novella evaporated. Let's not get hysterical.

I first taught *Mathilda* several years ago, when young adult literature was coming into its most gruesome manifestation—teenagers murdering each other on a reality show, vampire boyfriends displaying their sexy restraint as they try not to eat you, teenage cancer patients kissing in the Anne Frank house and then dying in a way I somehow didn't see coming, a way that left me crying on an airplane.

When Mary Shelley wrote *Mathilda*, she was twenty-two years old—not quite in the target demographic for YA lit but still, certainly, a YA.

In any case, my students loved it.

There's a woman in this coffee shop who ripped her leg open on a trail run and she is so proud of it. It's given her the chance to talk to half a dozen people about how she hurt herself trail running, but really is a mountain biker. I had my headphones in but I think I heard somebody say that his company might offer her some kind of product endorsement opportunity. I have also learned that, while she has been married twenty years—Maddy's fourteenth birthday party is today!—she thinks that those who use online dating websites should post photos of their worst falls and injuries, because that's "interesting." I want to dislike this woman, but I can't. I love how at home she is in her wound.

In contrast to Mary Shelley, I am sitting here writing about *Mathilda* while my father reads my son his favorite books dozens of times over. (Me: *just checking in*. Him: *all good; doing* Brown Bear.) It is for this reason I might never write a gothic masterpiece. Thanks a lot, Dad!

In 1943, sixteen years before her edition of *Mathilda* came out, Elizabeth Nitchie published a short article entitled "Mary Shelley's *Mathilda*: An Unpublished Story and Its Biographical Significance." In this article, describing a story most of her readers could not have read, Nitchie writes:

> *Mathilda* expresses a sense of estrangement from, even of physical repulsion toward, one whom she had deeply loved, a realization of her own selfish, petulant, and unreasoning absorption in her grief, and an acknowledgement that the man she loved, concealing or at least setting aside his own trouble, was unfailingly unselfish and kind—although, she felt, he did not love her. It contains other matters of interest too: references to her own birth and childhood, evidence of the attraction in the theme of incest for Mary as well as for Shelley, an expression of her feeling that she had "lost" her father by reason of his lack of sympathy toward her, and a portrait of Shelley comparable to those she was to draw of him again and again in her later fiction.[6]

On the "fanciful setting" mentioned above, Nitchie explains, "To make the heroine's description of her own death plausible, Mary experimented with an opening section and a closing paragraph which set Mathilda's tale as the narrative of a soul in the Elysian Fields waiting to be purged of her selfishness before she was permitted to rejoin the soul of her father . . . Mary discarded this opening, however, and wrote another . . . in which the heroine, knowing that she is about to die, is sitting at four o'clock on a winter day in her cottage on the heath beginning to write out her tragic history for the benefit of her friend."[7] It's an interestingly pragmatic interpretation, Nitchie's, i.e., that Mary Shelley's initial conceptualization of the posthumous narrator was a matter of making the story "plausible," that the supernatural frames the natural for us, prefaces reality. But what can we make of the ghost in the story, the ghost Mary Shelley edits out?

Regarding this redacted frame narrative, E. B. Murray explains, "While Nitchie is probably right when she states in her Introduction . . . that the title, setting, and framework of *The Fields of Fancy* 'stem from Mary Wollstonecraft's unfinished tale, *The Cave of Fancy*,' in which a dead heroine tells a tale of woe incipiently kindred to the one told by Mathilda,

Mary Shelley had herself previously written the beginning of a tale told
in the same locale . . . and of course Shelley himself had earlier begun a
similar tale in a work he entitled *The Elysian Fields*. The framework . . .
is in itself an attractive piece of fancified Platonism (Diotema is the narrator's guide), stylistically and ideologically more reminiscent of Shelley
than of Mary, which is perhaps one reason why it was dispensed with,
though others are readily inferable."[8]

How might we reconcile form and process? How square *Mathilda*'s
immediacy with its history of erasure? Tilottama Rajan explains that, in
contrast to *Frankenstein*, where "multiple narratives frame and reframe
[the novel's] central horror so as to keep open the (im)possibility of
explaining and overcoming trauma,"

> *Mathilda* . . . discloses in its very textual history a resistance to the
> logic of incorporation inscribed in the gesture of framing. In its first
> version as *The Fields of Fancy*, the text is prefaced by an interlude in
> the Elysian fields where an extradiegetic narrator who has also suf-
> fered some misfortune is led to the Prophetess Diotima, among whose
> disciples is Mathilda, whom Diotima calls upon to narrate "her earthly
> history." By interpellating Mathilda into a Platonic and Dantesque *bil-
> dung*, and by implying an instructional hierarchy that descends from
> Diotima through Mathilda to a narrator who represents the reader, the
> original frame conventionalizes suffering as purgatorial. This appara-
> tus of temporal and narratorial distancing, which mimes what one
> is supposed to do in shaping "life" into "art," is entirely dropped in
> *Mathilda*. Echoes of Dante remain, but instead of being incorporated
> into the text's structure, they survive only on the level of affect, where
> they protect a desire for idealization that the text is unable to use.[9]

In seminar, poet Ashley Colley refers to Mathilda's habitual "retreat into
the classical body"; literary history is a body we can animate, if we like.
It's a place we can, I guess, dwell. But if genre is always historically determined, can breaking the rules of genre undermine the rules we expect
history to obey?

In the discarded frame narrative, Mathilda overhears "Diotima" telling a
"beauteous girl":

> It is true indeed she said our affections out live our earthly forms
> and I can well sympathize in your dissappoint ment [*sic*] that you

do not find what you loved in the life now ended to welcome you here But one day you will all meet how soon entirely depends upon yourself—.[10]

This is on a page the entirety of which is crossed out.

Nitchie approximates that Mary Shelley wrote *Mathilda* between August 4 and September 12, 1819, with some final revisions in November.[11] We recall that William Shelley died on June 7 and Percy Florence was born on November 12 of that year. *You will all meet* is a mother's impossible wish.

In Wollstonecraft's fragment *The Cave of Fancy*, an old sage, who has undertaken a young girl's education, studies her mother's dead body on the beach:

> Anxious to observe the mother of his charge, he turned to the lily that had been so rudely snapped, and, carefully observing it, traced every fine line to its source. There was a delicacy in her form, so truly feminine, that an involuntary desire to cherish such a being, made the sage again feel the almost forgotten sensations of his nature . . . the fine finish of her features, and particularly the form of the forehead, convinced / the sage that her understanding might have risen considerably above mediocrity, had the wheels ever been put in motion.[12]

The mother's face, considered in the light of physiognomy, becomes a map of society's failings, a map of collective desires. On ghosts, Mary Shelley writes:

> For my own part, I never saw a ghost except once in a dream. I feared it in my sleep; I awoke trembling, and lights and the speech of others could hardly dissipate my fear.[13]

Commenting on a draft of this essay, Stephanie Hershinow asked, *Can you help me get from the missed opportunities of corpses back to ghosts? Between corporeality and incorporeality? Form and formlessness or form's shadow?* And it read like a theory of form I could get behind, a theory of literature as an embodied channel, a tracing back to or toward the source.

Now that I'm a mother, I finally understand ghosts. Mary Shelley writes, "There is something beyond us of which we are ignorant. The sun drawing up the vaporous air makes a void, and the wind rushes in to fill it . . . it bestows on the feeling heart a belief that influences do exist to watch and guard us, though they be impalpable to the coarser faculties."[14] Referring to her three-year-old, Rufi Thorpe writes, "It is my job to be invisible to him."[15] This is another edge to maternal erasure—the way my son wants me and only me at four in the morning, but will take any more exciting human delight come four in the afternoon. The way I evacuate my ego, finding my calling as that "impalpable" force that exists to "watch and guard" him, because all I care about, really all I fucking care about, is what happens in and to his "feeling heart." Paraphrasing Judith Viorst, my mother says that if you ask any small child, *would you rather have mommy away and happy or crying in the kitchen?* he will choose the kitchen scenario, every time.[16]

The night after the second presidential debate, I awoke with a start, sure a man was standing over my bed. That this man was permitted to debate this woman—to skulk after her across the stage—days after a tape surfaced in which he bragged about committing sexual assault struck fear into my heart. Or is there another explanation? Mary Shelley edits Mary Wollstonecraft's ghost out of *Mathilda*. So perhaps she came here, instead, to haunt me and to wake me up.

In the absence of the frame narrative, Mathilda begins and concludes her tale on her "solitary, wide heath."[17] She writes, "you are the sole tie that binds me to existence, and now I break it . . . You never regarded me as one of this world, but rather as a being, who for some penance was sent from the Kingdom of Shadows; and she passed a few days weeping on the earth . . ."[18]

Mathilda sits in joyous anticipation of the life about to leave her body. In this way, her death is not unlike a scene of childbirth. To William, who has died, and to Percy Florence, who has yet to be born, Mathilda confesses: "your heart is the only tomb in which my memory will be interred."[19]

13

Unearthly

Every story is a story of abandonment. Even *The Cat in the Hat*. And every story of abandonment is a story of discovery or rediscovery.

Mathilda is sixteen when her father reappears; it is like a birth. She becomes lost in the woods on her way to greet him, then finds a skiff and parts the waters:

> As I came, dressed in white, covered only by my tartan *rachan*, my hair streaming on my shoulders, and shooting across with greater speed than it could be supposed I could give to my boat, my father has often told me that I looked more like a spirit than a human maid. I approached the shore, my father held the boat, I leapt lightly out, and in a moment was in his arms.
> And now I began to live.[1]

Mathilda goes on to explain, "I felt as if I were recreated and had about me all the freshness and life of a new being: I was, as it were, transported since his arrival from a narrow spot of earth into a universe boundless to the imagination and the understanding."[2]

I pushed for so long, your head was a sausage, a link in the chain, alien. They threw you on my chest; I do not think you cried. I looked and spotted the dimple on your nose, a tiny imperfection, an open pore. Survival. *I know which one is mine*, I thought as the blood continued to pour out of me, *the one with the dot on his nose. Dot on his nose.* And everything went black.

Your father held the boat, and you leapt lightly out, and you were in his arms, and you began to live.

An ark is a clumsy kind of machine and so is a mother.

Describing his sixteen-year separation from his abandoned daughter, Mathilda's father recounts a kind of prenatal anxiety. A letter to his sister announcing his impending arrival explains, "'I cannot tell you . . . how ardently I desire to see my Mathilda. I look on her as the creature who will form the happiness of my future life: she is all that exists on earth that interests me.'"[3] Reunited with Mathilda, he tells her, "my fervent hopes were dashed by so many fears; my impatience became in the highest degree painful. I dared not think that the sun should shine and the moon rise not on your livid form but on your grave."[4] Sarah Allison describes pregnancy as a thrumming sentence: *please be alive, please be alive, please be alive.*

Mathilda's description of her new relationship with her father reads like a primer on infant attachment. "We were forever together."[5] "He was now all love, all softness: and when I raised my eyes in wonder at him as he spoke the smile on his lips told me that his heart was possessed by the gentlest passions."[6] "The tender attachment that he bore me, and the love and veneration with which I returned it cast a charm over every moment"; "I was always happy when near my father."[7]

He was all love. A description of the father's temperament, to be sure, but also the insistence that he is all and only love, that the parent to whom one attaches is the source of all love, past present future. In class, a group of students claim the father and Woodville are each sometimes the father and sometimes the son, but Mathilda is always the holy ghost.[8]

Today is your birthday. It is the day I bear, the day I bore. Last night, on *60 Minutes*, a man swore to overturn *Roe v. Wade*. Today, I'm thinking about Mathilda, unwanted and then badly wanted, but badly, the wrong way, Mathilda who regrets that she was ever born and dies. Last night, we sat on the porch with dear friends. They were discussing possible paths to parenthood, explaining that *they say it's never a good time . . . OK, that's true, if you're straight. But if you're two guys, it takes so long, and it's so expensive . . .*

The supermoon came out, daring to come closer than she has in years, emboldened, perhaps, by the *fuck-it phase of grief.* You pointed upward, saying, *ball, ball, ball.*

I am your mother every day but today the channel was open. Yesterday we sang to you, your little friends were there, their moccasins. You waited for me to crouch down with the cake, a yogic squat; you wanted to touch the flame.

My brother said, *he can tell it's his party, but then, when is it not his party?*

To be a mother is to be in the business of world creation, which is a glorified term for event planning.

Once, in a prenatal yoga class, the instructor explained that, while she'd always planned on being an "attachment parent," her first child (Phoenix!) was not an "attachment son." He didn't want to be bound to her with organic gauze; he didn't care to sleep in her bed; he wanted her to put him down by the window. As a toddler, he explained: *Mommy, I'm just not a close guy.*

You, my love, are the opposite. I want you in the safest crib, a firm little mattress, a colorful sheet, a nontoxic finish on the dusted wood. *Let's lie down in the crib,* I explained to you, once. (I'm ashamed, now, to write it.) *That's where babies sleep.*

Babies sleep with their mommies! Your father laughed. Essentially, it comes down to SIDS risk vs. cultural relativism. How proximate you are to the down comforter/rescue pit bull/attached parent when I let my mind leave my body.

Of her father, Mathilda writes, "I wondered how he could ever again have entered into the offices of life after his wild thoughts seemed to have given him affinity with the unearthly; while he spoke so tremendous were the ideas which he conveyed that it appeared as if the human heart were far too bounded for their conception."[9] She's explaining her sense of her father after her mother's death; this means, of course, after her own birth. What might we make of this metaphor—the human heart too bounded for the conception of his ideas? His affinity with the unearthly, his love for the dead, will, we know, lead to a dark passion that taints Mathilda's sense of self and of her futurity. Because of this affinity with the unearthly, his heart is unbounded, not meat in his meat machine, but released for conception, the egg falling down the ovarian tube, wondering, the heart a relic, the heart a ghost, the heart harvested, collected.

When I first sensed you within me, I imagined a little girl. I called her Rose—I have letters I wrote to you, very early on in my pregnancy, that begin, *dear Rose.*

When the ultrasound technician said, *it's a little boy* (as opposed to a big boy?), I asked your father if he could believe it, and he said, *yes, of course I can believe it.*

I imagined you as a little Rose, I told him, after the technician finished tracing your organs, because, when I imagined parenthood, I didn't think of changing diapers or rocking you to sleep. I imagined showing you *Dirty Dancing* for the first time, which, of course, I will still do. Your father somehow had not seen it, and so that weekend we watched it, a big bowl of popcorn by the big bowl of my belly. And none of this is a good way to say what I will say only once or as often as necessary: that no person should have to grow and bear a child who does not want to. Because, man, let me tell you: even when you want to.

Winnicott writes that mothers "develop an amazing capacity for identification with the baby, and this makes them able to meet the basic needs of the infant in a way that no machine can imitate, and no teaching can reach."[10] On Mathilda, he writes, "An infant who is held well enough is quite a different thing from one who has not been held well enough."[11] Of the aunt who takes her in when her father decides to peace out, Mathilda explains, "I believe that without the slightest tinge of a bad heart she had the coldest that ever filled a human breast: it was totally incapable of any affection."[12] As opposed to the father's heart (unbounded, akin to the unearthly), Mathilda's aunt's heart fills her breast like a frozen Butterball turkey, a slab of meat in the ice chest.

These hearts, these hearts. These hearts forced into the lungs, the liver, the armpit without consent. The inability of a small book about Mary Shelley to influence a Supreme Court appointment, a Supreme Court ruling. My little book, my little boy.

Like Victor Frankenstein, Mathilda's father abandons the infant. Where Frankenstein rediscovers the neglected creature with unbounded hate, Mathilda's father encounters his daughter with poisonously boundless love. When Johnny leaves, he says *I'll never be sorry.* Baby's hinged at the waist, her head to his chest; she looks up and says *neither will I.*[13] You lifted the toy train up so I could see it. *Boat,* you explained.

Today at the pediatrician's office, we were giving you a bottle, the pediatrician asked *doesn't he hold his own bottle?*

She told you, *hold your own bottle!* (Then she said, *it's just the cutest thing, that dimple on his nose.*)

I decided you were perhaps too old for bottles. We went shopping for cups, whole milk. We waited in line patiently, you holding a piece of melon and showing it to some college girls, your side-eye glance, their smiles. When we finally made it to the front of the line, a man barged in from the opposite direction. He thought the line started over there. He thought I was waiting in the line wrong. And anyway, he only had this roast beef, which he held up like a small fowl just slain and lifted from the mouth of a dog. I said no words. No words! And after he paid, I paid. The cashier, the kind of person I now think of as *a nice young man*, said, *thanks for doing that.* I said, *it's almost never worth it.* You chewed the fake pen one uses to forge an electronic signature.

Why am I telling you this? Because you are seeing, already, how easy some men find it to dismiss a woman.

There is an email listserv for North American Romanticists, and it is mostly great, especially when scholars accidentally hit "reply all" and include juicy gossip and snide remarks. It sometimes also provides a framework within which to claim that Mary Shelley did not write *Frankenstein*. (We all have our internet trolls, even Mary Shelley.) Now, to be fair, on some level, it is true that Percy Shelley wrote *Frankenstein*—the level on which my work is written by your father, and your father's work is written by me, because our marriage represents a sustained intellectual collaboration.[14]

Today, on the listserv, someone wrote, *I have already posted too often on this topic, yet the obvious point never sinks in . . . many dozens of readers have been convinced that Mary Shelley was incapable of writing* Frankenstein, *and that Percy Bysshe Shelley is the true author.* A follow-up email referred to the *Mary Shelley myth.*[15]

It may seem like I'm comparing this person to the roast beef person but that is too simplistic. I would not call his theory feminist but we are all entitled to our theories, our arguments, our disagreements with the establishment.

But *why* does this always get such a rise out of people on the listserv? They mock, they insist, they dismiss. As if a wrong idea isn't an honorable thing, in its own strange way.

Every story, after all, is a story of abandonment.

And here is what I want to say: of course Mary Shelley was "incapable" of writing *Frankenstein*. None of us are capable of our best works. This is exactly what *Frankenstein* suggests—you can't build your progeny with your hands and your mind. You can't make life from books. The life goes through you—your life, his life. A book can be like that, too. If you let it, it can all be like that—all of life can be like that.

But Mathilda's father disrupts the order of things. He doesn't hold her at all, and then he holds her too tightly. She waits, and then she comes to him, "shooting across [the water] with greater speed *than it could be supposed I could give* to my boat."[16] Her hair, streaming behind her. Her mother's life and death behind her. The precise, astonishing stroke of the oars parting the loch.

14

Under the Sign

"Blood" turns out to be an important word in *The Cenci*: referring to both kinship and wounds. And it was his blood's muscle that would outlive Percy in both senses. Percy's dead body was supposed to be completely burned on the beach where he washed up, but the heart remained unburned and was given to Mary. She spent the remainder of her life with it, living with and defending the rights of Percy Florence, her dead husband's only surviving child. When Mary died in 1851, the heart was buried with her.

— Barbara Johnson, *Mary Shelley and Her Circle*

Reading Toni Morrison's *Sula*, Nella Larsen's *Passing*, and the films *Thelma and Louise* and *The Accused* in an attempt to find "a way of catching myself in the act of reading as a lesbian without having intended to," Barbara Johnson refers to her "inner lesbometer" as well as her "attempt to view [the films] through lesbian spectacles."[1] Such turns of phrase are enough to make me imagine a tattoo that says *Barbara Johnson Forever.*

I have been reading the news through some old spectacles. Every mention of a swastika through the same old spectacles. When my mother's father was a very young boy, he was hidden in a barn; if we must, we will hide in a barn, and if not, then we will hide those who must hide in our barn. A mother is like an ark, which is not unlike a barn. God said to Noah, get some wood and nails and a hammer, or something. Get the job done.

Ultimately, Johnson writes that she "[has] to conclude that the project of making my own erotic unconscious participate in my reading process, far from guaranteeing some sort of radical or liberating breakthrough, brings me face to face with the political incorrectness of my own fantasy life."[2] She writes:

> Any attempt to go on from this reading to theorize (my) lesbian desire would therefore have to confront the possibility of a real disjunction between my political ideals and my libidinal investments. But if the unconscious is structured by repetition and the political by the desire for change, there is nothing surprising about this.[3]

Although admittedly my conundrum is less interesting, this resonates with me. Reading Mary Shelley, *Frankenstein*, and *Mathilda* as a mother drives me to methodological innovation, to the sparse and frantic and lyrical, to the reading that breaks the rules. But it has also hastened my return to a very traditional genre: the book-length, feminist reading of Mary Shelley. (The short book, even. The *readable* book.) And it has ignited a fascination with that which is out of fashion: psychoanalytical criticism, reader response(ish) criticism, a return to author studies not particularly aligned with more prescriptive examples from the "new author studies." In "My Monster/My Self," Johnson argues that "the monstrousness of selfhood is intimately embedded within the question of female autobiography . . . The problem for the female autobiographer is, on the one hand, to resist the pressure of masculine autobiography as the only literary genre available for her enterprise, and, on the other, to describe a difficulty in conforming to a female ideal which is largely a fantasy of the masculine, not the feminine, imagination."[4]

Working thesis: Mary Shelley, or, at least, the Mary Shelley we have today, is largely a fantasy of the feminist imagination.

Barbara Johnson finished *Mary Shelley and Her Circle*—last book, brief book, posthumously published book—with one finger, the rest of her hands required to hold herself up and steady in front of the computer monitor.[5] Thus, Shoshana Felman writes, "Johnson's body seems to be inscribed in the margin of her final manuscript, particularly in the abbreviated, gasping, racing, almost breathless textuality of her final pages. It is as though Johnson had written the ungraspable physical event of the imminent interruption of her life and writing into her last manuscript."[6]

I love the image these statements conjure, in contrast to one another—of language, identity, feminism, not as something that can be *grasped*, held tight in the hand, but rather as that which we press forward, one letter at a time, all our digits, all our prints, used to right ourselves, to write, ourselves, to steady our vision.

This is what I have committed to, in the weeks following the election. I am not saying that it is enough.

This book, the one Johnson pecked out, offers a rereading of Romanticism itself. Felman writes, "Romanticism is presumed to be the language of the heart. Yet in *Mary Shelley and Her Circle*, Romanticism rewrites itself as the language—the enigma—of the charred heart."[7]

In *Mary Shelley and Her Circle*, on the topic of Wollstonecraft's fiction, Johnson writes:

> With all the prison imagery of the gothic novel and the marriage laws, with the efforts to find a place for unruly emotions, there is one thing Mary Wollstonecraft left out, and that was the thing that, in the end, she died from. In the gothic novel, women are often confined . . . But the most telling instance of "confinement to bed," the most indicative of sexual difference, was childbearing.[8]

In "My Monster/My Self," Johnson calls *Frankenstein* "a tale of motherless birth" and calls Mary Shelley "the unwitting murderous intruder present on her own parents' wedding night: their decision to marry was due to the fact that Mary Wollstonecraft was already carrying the child that was to kill her . . . what [*Frankenstein*] suggests is that what is at stake behind what is currently being banalized under the name of female fear of success is nothing less than the fear of somehow effecting the death of one's own parents."[9]

Felman's afterword to *Mary Shelley and Her Circle*—which is, at once, an elegy and a theory of feminist reading—includes these thoughts on reading and birth and death:

> Mary meets death even while she is born, through the loss of her own mother, who dies in giving birth to her, and whom she consequently will never know except as a living and dead ghost, in the actual ghost story of her life. She then lives through the unexpected death in

infancy of three of the four children she has borne, of whom only one
survives into maturity . . . Johnson in turn meets death early on . . .

"Reading is a form of friendship," Proust has written. "And the
fact that it is directed at someone who is dead, who is not there, lends
something disinterested, almost moving, to it." Through the bond of
reading she creates with Mary Shelley so as to articulate for her sister-
writer Mary's own impossible autobiography, Johnson understands
that the writing competition which starts as a shared bid for female
authorship and for feminine equality, ultimately turns into a much
more primordial, existential struggle between life and death.

But each one of the women writers thus knotted in this bond of
reading lives her fate—confronts death—in a different way.[10]

Every act of reading is an act of demystification, which is a fancy word
for friendship. But there is something so beautiful, here, about that compound word: *sister-writer*. It contains within its dash a whole theory of
elective affinities. According to Felman, Johnson writes Shelley's "impossible autobiography." But, in a way, doesn't Felman do the same for
Johnson? *Mary Shelley and Her Circle* is ultimately published, along with
essays and gloss, as *A Life with Mary Shelley*. Felman writes that, despite
"inner divisions" and conceptual "fissure[s]" in feminism:

> in placing her last work again under the sign of Mary Shelley, John-
> son's final message is still obstinately feminist, still understatedly
> affirmative of a struggle toward a greater justice and a greater free-
> dom. Johnson as the narrator of *Mary Shelley and Her Circle*—and
> her questioning—are inhabited by a sense of contradiction, a sense of
> radical impossibility, yet are also driven by a passion for the impos-
> sible. Johnson claims (for Mary Shelley, for herself, for feminists, for
> humans) a right to contradiction, a "right to ambivalence." The writ-
> ing's act of affirmation—*countering the contradiction*—is enabled
> thanks to literature, whose promise and desire is to liberate, to set
> us free.[11]

Mary Shelley, then, can affirm our messy feminism and promise us a relationship to the impossible and "set us free." She is a ghost in the "real"
ghost story of our lives. This, according to Felman, is feminism "under
the sign of Mary Shelley," that is, feminism via elective affinity with a
nineteenth-century woman who could not write her own "impossible
autobiography," feminism via friendship, friendship that transcends history, genre, nation.

In her trademark style, Johnson's take on Mary Shelley, birth, and death is all wit and vinegar. She is not dead yet, and does not yet talk of liberation:

> Mary had many children by Percy, in fact. She was pregnant five times [Clara, William, Clara Everina, Percy Florence, and a miscarriage] by the age of twenty-five. After Harriet's death, Percy sought custody of their two children, but was not awarded it because of his atheism and his unorthodox lifestyle. Although Mary thought this unfair, she did not think Percy took parenthood as seriously as a mother needed to. When her daughter Clara Everina died after a rapid journey to Venice, where Percy, staying with Byron, had called them, Mary blamed Percy for their daughter's death. And when William, Percy's son and heir, died a few months later in the region of Italy the family had moved to partly for Percy's health, Mary was disconsolate. Percy thought she mourned too long, and she resented him for that, too. So she was mad at him for several things when he drowned in 1822. And though she was in deep mourning, his death had two empowering effects on her: she looked good in black, and, while a living husband could always be unfaithful, there could only be one official widow.[12]

In *Mother Tongues*, Johnson writes: "Motherhood seems in our culture to connote the very opposite of violence—a recourse against it and a refuge from it . . . There may be something inherent in the ideal that makes it violent in itself."[13] She writes: "The very exclusion of violence is itself violent"; and, "We never stop being a child. Only mothers are supposed to subordinate themselves entirely to the needs of someone else . . . Psychoanalytic theories allow for violence toward or from the father, but the taboo on thinking about violence emanating from or performed by the mother is very strong. That taboo underlies the opposition to legal abortion in the United States."[14]

I expected this reception. What Frankenstein's creature tells the male mother who threatens to kill him.[15]

All of this is very dark, but then, Mary Shelley looked good in black, and so did Barbara Johnson, and so do I. In *A Life's Work*, Rachel Cusk recounts a moment in which her daughter falls but wants to be comforted by her father. Cusk writes, "I remain surprised by how proximate the mythology of motherhood is to its reality . . . *You came from my body!* I wanted to say. I was offering her what I had craved often in my life, another body in which to be absorbed, enfolded, enclosed, an element in which to be reincorporated, and she didn't want it."[16]

I am not sure if I want to say that literature is the ghost in the real ghost story of our lives. Cusk writes, "Mothers are the countries we come from"; so are novels.[17] But why is *Frankenstein* the country my feminism comes from? And why and how do I make space for myself as a mother *there*, instead of somewhere else?

Felman's gloss on Johnson—like every feminist reading of Mary Shelley— reveals the false separation we make between our intellectual and our biological histories. As Johnson tells us, we view the film through twinned spectacles—what turns us on, and what we want to turn us on.

Late in my pregnancy, in the heavy afternoons, you would become still and I would become sleepy. I'd eat a peanut butter and jelly sandwich and drink a glass of juice. I'd think of all the millions upon millions of times I hoped to make this for you, a simple, childhood meal, nationless, banal. But you were inside me, and so I'd feed me instead, then make my way to the orange daybed in the window, and lie on my side, my fingers spread like fans across my belly, and the sugar would hit my blood, and wake you up, and you'd press with your elbow, and with what must have been a free foot, and I would count to ten—ten movements, ten pulses from you my daily meditation. Sometimes, if I tapped lightly, you'd tap back, the sugared imitation, all sweetness and nothing that sweetness implies, the blood-red jam. On Mary Shelley's fiction, a dying Barbara Johnson writes, "In Mary's novel *Frankenstein*, the monster kills off the family of his creator for lack of good parenting."[18] She writes, "most women have only fathers, never mothers."[19]

15

Catastrophe

This newfound love, this holding of Mathilda by her father and of the father by his daughter, cannot last long. In fact, it lasts nine months. After their reunion, Mathilda tells us, "Three months passed away in this delightful intercourse, when my aunt fell ill. I passed a whole month in her chamber nursing her . . . Two months after my aunt's death we removed to London."[1] Explaining the sudden change from her father's warm happiness to his cold misery, Mathilda tells us, "We had remained five months in London, three of joy and two of sorrow."[2] There's a pregnant period during which anything is possible. Then: the birth of the monster.

This monster—the father who cannot show love at all because he realizes the love he feels is all wrong—causes Mathilda to experience "a horror that will not bear many words, and I sink almost a second time to death while I recall these sad scenes to my memory."[3] Almost a second time—when is the first time? The moment of writing within an almost-posthumous frame narrative, or the moment of revelation?

Winnicott writes, "One of the things that father does for his children is to be alive and to stay alive during the children's early years."[4] He offers a counter-example:

> I knew a girl whose father died before she was born. The tragedy here
> was that she had only an idealized father on whom to base her view
> of man. She had not the experience of being let down gently by a real
> father. In her life she easily imagined men to be ideal, which at first
> had the effect of bringing out the best in them. But sooner or later,
> inevitably, each man she got to know showed imperfections, and each
> time this happened she was thrown into a state of despair, and contin-
> ually complaining. As you can imagine, this pattern ruined her life.[5]

See? He ruined her life, just by *dying*. Imagine if he had disappeared, leaving behind a romantic/Romantic letter, then reappeared, then given her nine months of bliss, then suddenly turned so that she "who sought and had found joy in the love-breathing countenance of my father now when I dared fix on him a supplicating look it was ever answered by an angry frown."[6] And my students wonder why Mathilda can't get over it, why she feels poisoned, fakes her death, longs for death, dies.

On the other hand, I am left wondering about the nature and degree of these "imperfections," and whether we must blame this woman's "complaining" on her dead father, and not on the men she dated. Furthermore, I do not necessarily imagine that this "pattern" ruined her life.

My mother, misspeaking about the dog, who cannot find his water dish, because I have moved it, because the baby loves to tip it over: *you brought an animal into this world*. Mary Wollstonecraft, going into labor with Mary Shelley: "I have no doubt of seeing the animal to day."[7]

Skimming through her pain, Mathilda tells us, "To tell all my grief I might as well attempt to count the tears that have fallen from these eyes, or every sign that has torn my heart."[8] "Sign" might be an error in Nitchie's transcription, and Michelle Faubert corrects it to "sigh" in her forthcoming edition, which will soon, I think, become the standard edition.[9] But my copy—purple—is the copy I have lived and travelled with, and so this possible error has shifted my reading. A sigh is just air because the horror cannot bear many words but a sign is an index, an indication, the tilt of the head, a shift in the weight on the leg so two legs that were touching no longer quite touch.

If *Frankenstein* is a birth myth, then *Mathilda* is a birth myth, too, nine months of closeness followed by overwhelming love and rejection. Only now, we know who the monster is.

Well, *we* might, but Mathilda doesn't, not yet. Her heart's still in it. She quotes a misogynistic play: "whose kindly heat / Should give my poor heart life."[10] Her heart is "torn" and, even then, her father "possess[es] [her] whole heart." He takes her back to his Yorkshire estate, where he lived with her mother before the birth/death. A servant recounts those happy days, and Mathilda's "heart was almost broken." Her father's eyes, "dark deep orbs so liquid and intense that even in happiness I could never meet their full gaze that mine did not overflow," seem to desire "a heart patient to suffer." Mathilda blames herself for his ultimate death and downfall because, rather than leave him alone in his misery and let time run its course, she pushes him to "confide his misery to another heart."[11]

And so Mathilda brings things to a crisis. Her "heart beat fast" as she "worked [herself] up to speak to him." She tells him he must listen, because her "heart is bursting"; she insists that her "heart is overflowing" with the desire to bring him peace. Her father tells her to back off, explaining, "In the heart of one like me there are secret thoughts working, and secret tortures which you ought not to seek to discover." She's insistent, though: "my whole heart is in the words I speak and you must not endeavour to silence me by mere words barren of meaning." Mathilda's father's words are "barren"; her words are pregnant, carrying her heart.[12]

What mothers say to explain why they worry: *you're walking around carrying my heart in your hands*. Or, to say I love you: *you have my heart*.

Mathilda's father doesn't want to spill the beans, doesn't want to implicate Mathilda in his criminal mind. At this point, the redundant metaphor becomes quite gruesome: "Much happier would it be for you and for me if in your frantic curiosity you tore my heart from my breast and tried to read its secrets in it as its life's blood was dropping from it." But Mathilda can't let it drop: "In despair of my heart I see what you cannot conceal: you no longer love me . . . has not an unnatural passion seized upon your heart?" Mathilda's father can't take it anymore; he confesses his tormenting passion. He tells his daughter, "my blood riots through my veins" and begs her, "Let me lay my head near your heart; let me die in your arms."[13]

This is quite the heart to heart! As opposed to the creator/creature (monster/monster) dynamic in *Frankenstein*, in which the horrible appearance of the creature first disguises who the true monster is, and then leads society to convince the creature that he must be a monster, too, here the surface is stripped away. It's all hearts and blood and veins, placental, gory exchange. As Mathilda's father says, she rips his heart from his chest, she divines his desires in the very blood, because her blood rises to match his blood.[14]

This makes sense, of course, in an incest plot—Mathilda and her father cannot or will not commingle their blood because they are already bound by blood. But what of their beating hearts?

Regina Spektor sings, *never mind your beating heart*.[15] Good advice, for
Mathilda, if two centuries too late.

In the midst of his confession, Mathilda's father says, "Monster as I am,
you are still, as you ever were, lovely, beautiful beyond expression."[16] The
key word here is not *monster*, but *as*. Apply a little pressure to the syntax.
*Even though I am a monster, you are still lovely and beautiful. You are still
lovely and beautiful, even though you are a monster, like me. Frankenstein*
and *Mathilda* suggest that the child of a monster will become a monster, no matter how hard he/she tries to escape this fate, unless he/she is
adopted by someone else—the De Lacey family, an aunt who knows how
to hug, etc. This seems like the wrong lesson, but what can we do. Anne
Mellor thinks *Mathilda* is about Mary Shelley's complicated relationship
with Godwin, instigated, in part, by his dismissive comments following
her son's death. I'm not completely on board with this interpretation, but
if we follow Mellor's logic, we see an anxiety crystallize—if my parent is a
monster, then am I a monster, too? What then of the child within?[17]

Summing up *Mathilda*, which she has decided not to discuss at length,
Muriel Spark writes:

> It is a melodramatization of Mary Shelley's deepest feelings of hope-
> lessness following the death of her son William. She had borne three
> children and lost all, and was pregnant again. Her relations with
> Shelley were strained. Her father, whom she had idolized, was dun-
> ning the Shelleys for money; to him, Mary's feelings did not count.
> Three years later, after Shelley's death, Mary wrote in her journal,
> ". . . when I wrote Matilda miserable as I was, the *inspiration* was
> enough to quell my wretchedness temporarily . . ."[18]

Spark goes on to link *Mathilda* to *The Cenci* and to think about the
Romantic incest plot; I want to focus, instead, on the word *inspiration*,
literally, "breathing in." Sometimes you need to get out of your heart and
into your lungs. Sarah Manguso writes, "There should be extra days, buf-
fer days, between the real days."[19]

The night of the election, I let you sleep in the bed. I tried to sleep, one
hand on you and one hand on my tightening chest.

After her father's confession, Mathilda passes a fitful night in her room.
She feels "oppression of heart"; she dreams that someday her father

might be so old that his "heart [will be] chilled" and thus beat "with sin-less emotion." At one point, steps approach her door; she holds very still, and remarks on "the burning hell that consumed [her father's] heart" as well as how her "own heart beat with violent fear." She sleeps, experi-ences nightmares, and when she wakes her "heart beat[s] hard." A servant reports that her father has departed, and gives her a letter, which she begins to read "with a beating heart." The letter opens with the father's acknowledgment that he has "made your innocent heart acquainted with the looks and language of unlawful and monstrous passion." The letter that follows is all about his heart—its "overflowing anguish," its burn-ing disorder, that which has "filled" it "in quietness," the warmth that was extinguished in it, the warmth that was not extinguished in it, the "secrets" that "agonized" it, the grief he tried to reawaken in it by return-ing to the estate, the question of whether pain can "purify" it.[20]

Mathilda's dead mother, Diana, was "the life of [Mathilda's father's] life"; she "filled up all his heart."[21] She filled up all his heart, and took it over, and grew Mathilda's heart within her with her husband's blood, and bore her in blood, and died. The mother is a harvester of hearts. And in her wake: just hearts.

16

Created

Ellen Moers is the first to argue that, while "Mary Shelley said she intended *Frankenstein* to be the kind of ghost story that would 'curdle the blood, and quicken the beatings of the heart,'" the novel is also "a birth myth, and one that was lodged in the novelist's imagination, I am convinced, by the fact that she was herself a mother."[1] (Moers made this argument in 1985, the year of my own birth.) From Moers's perspective, Shelley's experience of motherhood represents a unique character note:

> nothing so sets her apart from the generality of writers of her own time, and before, and for long afterward, than her early and chaotic experience, at the very time she became an author, with motherhood. Pregnant at sixteen, and almost constantly pregnant throughout the following five years; yet not a secure mother, for she lost most of her babies soon after they were born; and not a lawful mother, for she was not married—not at least when, at the age of eighteen, Mary Godwin began to write *Frankenstein*. So are monsters born.[2]

Moers clarifies that Shelley "rejoiced at becoming a mother and loved and cherished her babies as long as they lived." These are my favorite moments in Moers's seminal essay, which acted as a sort of doula for feminist reappraisals of Mary Shelley in general, and *Frankenstein* in particular:

. . . *a woman's mythmaking on the subject of birth* . . .

Birth is a hideous thing in Frankenstein, *even before there is a monster.*

. . . *the trauma of afterbirth* . . .

The sources . . . were surely the anxieties of a woman who, as daughter, mistress, and mother, was a bearer of death.

. . . phantasmagoria of the nursery . . .[3]

To be a bearer of death is to be a harvester of hearts, those hearts quickened, their blood curdled. I have quoted Moers in this scattered way because it is her turns of phrase that most appeal to me. (Her argument, at this point, has been naturalized, modifications and counterpoints registered.) Everyone quotes Moers's "birth myth," but what about "lodged in the novelist's imagination"? As if her experiences as a mother lifted up the idea for *Frankenstein* and punctured Mary Shelley's mind with it; as if her mind furnished a welcoming domicile for the horror story. On poetic inspiration, Jack Spicer famously said that an alien came into his head and rearranged the furniture.[4] I say *as if*, but these images do not feel untrue, at least to me. The confluence of book and baby have rendered my mind something not unlike a *phantasmagoria of the nursery*, a child-centered dreamscape of reception and strange colors—neon pink, pale peach.

Pregnancy, in any case, is not unlike lodging an alien in one's body. In fact, that's exactly what it is.

In *Frankenstein*, the first words of Walton's frame narrative are "You will rejoice."[5] The first words of Frankenstein's tale are "I am by birth."[6] By birth: how we all are. What amazed me, walking around after giving birth, was the extent to which the world became a phantasmagoria of the nursery. *Somebody pulled that person from her body and kept that person alive*, an endless refrain lodged in my brain as my eyes met faces, met signs that said *hungry*. Every heart is a harvested heart.

If the downstairs neighbors are listening today, they have heard:

I respect your right to make many decisions about your body but the decision about whether or not to wear a diaper is not one of them . . .

. . . have you heard about this fetal-remains legislation in Texas . . .

. . . do you think he'll be mad, when he's a teenager, that I wrote about him as a baby . . .

. . . No, *this is the age of social media, none of his friends will have undocumented childhoods* . . .

And about an hour of *Anne of Green Gables* performed by Rachel McAdams. I have been returning to the songs of my youth, what my students call *90s music* and blast from their dorms ironically.

A colleague with a teenager said *it goes so fast* and I said *it makes everything go fast it's an accelerator.*

Of his creature's birth, Frankenstein tells Walton (and thus Margaret, thus you):

> It was on a dreary night of November, that I beheld the accomplishment of my toils. With an anxiety that almost amounted to agony, I collected the instruments of life around me, that I might infuse a spark of being into the lifeless thing that lay at my feet. It was already one in the morning; the rain pattered dismally against the panes, and my candle was nearly burnt out, when, by the glimmer of the half-extinguished light, I saw the dull yellow eye of the creature open; it breathed hard, and a convulsive motion agitated its limbs.[7]

It was on a dreary night in November that I made my way straight from a faculty meeting to a conference, dinner skipped, and out we slipped, a flood, flooding, floored.

I want to write about the creature's birth but everything has already been said and so I am writing about your birth but everything has already been said because, as Moers wrote a long time ago, it is a myth that has always already been lodged in my imagination.

With an anxiety that almost amounted to agony I pushed through my third trimester, my midsection so heavy I couldn't even take the stairs; every microwave, every coat of fresh paint, every too-old book felt poisonous. You'd go still in the afternoons—napping, I guess, in retrospect—and I'd worry if I couldn't rouse you. I couldn't see you. At those times I would sit in meditation.

Now you are at Whole Foods with your father, in your pajamas, yet another cliché.

To say this scene calls to mind Mary Shelley's dream of rubbing her dead daughter's feet and warming her and bringing her back to life is just about the least original thing I could say.

But, that little girl . . . that's a real little girl—or was, anyway. A girl who wrote nothing down. A girl I cannot recover.

Rose, I called you, too small to share, too small to be real. *You're barely pregnant,* the doctor told me. *It's not time to tell anyone yet.* What would it have mattered if I had? Why do we tell women this, imply that a miscarriage is something they shouldn't want to tell people about, something of which to be ashamed? Sometimes a body falls through like a word or a ghost. These children, too, are harvested hearts.

> How can I describe my emotions at this catastrophe, or how delineate the wretch whom with such infinite pains and care I had endeavoured to form? His limbs were in proportion, and I had selected his features as beautiful. Beautiful!—Great God! His yellow skin scarcely covered the work of muscles and arteries beneath; his hair was of a lustrous black, and flowing.[8]

Your hair, black from the beginning, the first thing I saw. This part, the part you'll be mad about, if I had to guess, when you're a teenager.

Frankenstein flees, and sleeps, or faints, and dreams, but darkly. When the creature reappears, he's acting like a one-year-old. (*It goes so quickly, doesn't it?*) "He held up the curtain of the bed . . . he muttered some inarticulate sounds, while a grin wrinkled his cheeks . . . one hand was stretched out, seemingly to detain me, but I escaped."[9] For Frankenstein and his creature, this moment of rejection is the beginning of the end.

Rivka Galchen describes the creature's early life as that of a toddler:

> Dr. Frankenstein [not a Dr.], the father (and mother) in a sense, notices the creature, shortly after creation, peering over the edge of a bed, like a toddler in his parents' room. Dr. Frankenstein flees in terror from the sight. The creature is then left on his own. For awhile he hangs around the house of a family he dreams of belonging to; the head of that family is a blind man; the creature one day gathers the courage to present himself to the kind, blind man; the man listens, sensitively, to the creature's story; then the man's children return,

scream in terror, and fight the "monster" off, even as said monster cries and clings to the knees of the blind father, as would a very young child.

After that [and other rejections], the creature becomes angry, and violent—also like a young child.

The creature eats only fruits and berries, and never meat.

Most people report that when seeing babies they have a desire to eat them.

So babies do appear in literature maybe more than we might first notice.[10]

Elsewhere in the book—after another mention of *Frankenstein*, in fact—Galchen writes, "We know babies are the only ones among us in alliance with time."[11] In a poem I have read at multiple weddings, Adam Zagajewski calls love and time "eternal enemies."[12] But what about motherhood and time? When the creature blinks to life, Frankenstein flees; he "travers[es] his bed chamber" until he can finally pass out, then "[throws himself] on the bed in [his] clothes, endeavouring to seek a few moments of forgetfulness."[13] In his "wildest dreams," which follow the collapse, Elizabeth walks around "in the bloom of health"; Frankenstein gives her a hug and a kiss, and she transforms from a hottie on a stroll in a sundress to his *mother*, "grave-worms crawling in the folds of the flannel" of her "shroud."[14] I'm gonna get really real with you for a second: substitute gummy worms for grave-worms and this is pretty accurate. Describing the creature, Walton explains, "one vast hand was extended, in colour and apparent texture like that of a mummy."[15]

So what do we do about motherhood as acceleration, besides write fast and listen to Third Eye Blind in an effort to hark back to a simpler time? What to do with a heartbeat set to warp speed?

You are tall, somehow, although we are not tall. You are reaching, rising up.

The "dull yellow eye" is your eye, by which I mean my eye. When I had you I woke up to time, its breakneck clip.

In "How's It Going to Be," Third Eye Blind sings, "how's it going to be / when you don't know me / how's it going to be / when you're sure I'm not there." They also claim, "'cause I don't care," which comes off as disaffected, ironic, but in the case of Victor Frankenstein is legit.[16] He doesn't realize that he doesn't get to know how it is going to be. He tries to make it be how it is going to be when the creature doesn't know him now, in the moment of birth, not the moment of death. But you can't know, which Mary Shelley must have known—in relation to Wollstonecraft, in relation to her little girl, in relation to her living children, who would die, in relation to the child she hadn't had yet, who would outlive her, in relation to the miscarriage that would almost kill her. Among other things, *Frankenstein* is about the monstrosity of not knowing.

In *Where the Wild Things Are*, the little boy is acting like a monster and so his mother treats him like a monster or like she is a monster and sends him to bed without his supper. His room in no way looks like the room of a little boy but it becomes the forest, the ocean, the land of monsters to which he travels within a span of time that makes no sense, "through night and day and in and out of weeks and almost over a year." When the little boy meets the monsters he "tame[s] them with the magic trick of staring into all their yellow eyes without blinking once."[17]

In Margaret Wise Brown's *Big Red Barn*, there are two piles of hay, "And that is where the children play. But in this story the children are away. Only the animals are here today." But night comes, and only the animals play, and finally "Only the mice were left to play, / Rustling and squeaking in the hay."[18] Anne E. Fernald has argued that Margaret Wise Brown is a modernist, and has revealed the literary- and intellectual-historical links between *Goodnight Moon* and Gertrude Stein.[19] (*Goodnight nobody!*) So, yes, Brown's books get us out of the self—enough to fall asleep! But where did the children go? And are they coming back? And why must they be away?

Wild things are fun but eventually, much like Frankenstein's creature, the little boy wants "to be where someone loved him best of all."[20]

Later, to a parent that has threatened to murder him, the creature narrates his own birth:

> "It is with considerable difficulty that I remember the original aera of my being: all the events of that period appear confused and indistinct. A strange multiplicity of sensations seized me, and I saw, felt, heard, and smelt, at the same time; and it was, indeed, a long time before I learned to distinguish between the operations of my various senses."[21]

Your father's talk was last, and he had worked so hard, and I guessed, rightly, that we had plenty of time. So I sent my mother for the car, and she said *I'll meet you at the spot*, by which she meant, the spot where she used to pick me up when I was eighteen—Mary Shelley's age when she started writing *Frankenstein*—and not yet in college but taking an introduction to philosophy class with a graduate student whose name I can't remember but who taught concepts so clearly I can conjure his explanations in a heartbeat.

To discuss the mind-body problem, he used the example of a CD. The disc itself is not Third Eye Blind's eponymous 1997 album but if you scratch the CD . . .

When your father called, I had already been (we had already been?) at the hospital for a couple of hours. I said *how'd it go* and he said *no you first*. Then three days of pain and trauma I barely remember. We put Christmas lights in the window like naive idiots. There was a moment before I began pushing when I could see the light breaking over the mountains and everything felt possible.

We went in there as one person but we came out as two, a strange multiplicity.

17

Mix

When *Hamilton* opens in Chicago, my brother's colleague lands the cellist gig; she gets us tickets the next time we're in town. This is after the show has become a site of protest and/or diversion. Despite my general aversion to liking things everybody else likes, I'm enraptured, and cry when Eliza Hamilton bends over the body of her dying son because even though it's a musical I can no longer, as they say, handle that shit.

There's a portrait of Mary Wollstonecraft hanging in the New York Public Library. It's John Keenan's copy of John Opie's painting; it was commissioned by Aaron Burr. I wanted to see it, but the room was being set up for a private event; the event staff sneaked me in. Everyone was lounging around in their bright vests, chatting, ready to circulate appetizers among who-knows-whom.

At a quieter moment in *Hamilton*, Aaron Burr sings to his daughter about the difficulty of addressing one's child. There are no child actors in the show, so he faces the audience, and, for a moment, we get to be Theodosia.

It's not easy being Theodosia.

Aaron Burr sings, *Dear Theodosia, what to say to you? You have my eyes. You have your mother's name.*

In other words, you have my bodily history as well as your mother's history of signification.

When you came into the world, you cried and it broke my heart.

The mother is a harvester of hearts. When she pulled your heart, which is her heart, from her body, she broke my heart, as well.

The song is hopeful, in general. We are Theodosia. We will *come of age with our young nation*, and, *someday*, we'll *blow* [them] *all away*.[1]

In a popular press article on *Hamilton*'s mischaracterization of Burr, historian Nancy Isenberg argues, "If the leftish audiences that have fallen for the play's energy and spirit want a genuine icon to look to, they should spend a little time getting to know its villain, whose reputation deserves to be recovered from the tabloid pages of history." Isenberg pays particular attention to Burr's attachment to Mary Shelley's mom:

> Burr was . . . advanced compared to his peers in terms of women's equality . . . Burr was far ahead of Hamilton, Jefferson and Adams in advancing the ideas of English philosopher Mary Wollstonecraft, the leading Enlightenment advocate of women's rights. Burr and his wife Theodosia educated their daughter as they might have a son: She could read and write by the age of 3, then mastered French, Italian, Latin, Greek, mathematics, history and geography.[2]

When Burr's political career fell apart (murder, disappearance into wilderness, trial for treason [acquitted but ruined]), he fled his debts to Europe, where he befriended Godwin and got to know a young Mary Shelley and bought her stockings. When he returned four years later to see his daughter (her son, his namesake, had died), the ship Theodosia took to meet him disappeared in the waters between Georgetown and New York City. The poor guy couldn't, as they say, catch a break.[3]

In the years just before his daughter's death, Aaron Burr's private journal includes a few mentions of a teenaged Mary Shelley. (Theodosia was in her late twenties when she died.) Burr writes, "At four to G.'s [Godwin's], to dine . . . Mary has come home, and looks very lovely, but has not the air of strong health"; and "Mr. Godwin, with Mary and Jane, came in and sat an hour"; and, "Called and passed an hour at the Godwins'. That family does really love me."[4] We know that Aaron Burr described Mary and her sisters as "extremely neat, and with taste" as they left for a ball.[5] We know that Burr heard little William Godwin (sorry, I know it's a lot of Williams) give a political speech and judged, probably correctly, that his half-sister had written it.[6]

Full disclosure: somebody once got their history wrong and told me Burr went to England following Theodosia's death and that, there, Mary Shelley became a sort of surrogate daughter to him. I know this was a mix-up, a false history, and cannot be used to understand Burr's relationship to the Godwin family in general and to little Mary Shelley in particular. I know I am sinning by committing this misspeak to university press paper. But much like the lyrics that convinced me Angelica Schuyler was an early feminist (Isenberg argues that Lin-Manuel Miranda conflates Angelica with Abigail Adams, and that "there is not a scintilla of evidence of such feminist leanings in either Mrs. or Mr. Hamilton, or his sister-in-law"[7]), I became convinced of this family romance, this fatherly substitution, and I cannot quite unlearn the false fact. Even stories that are not true can form the core of our intellectual history. Even lies give fire to our elective affinities.

Toward the end of *Hamilton*, Burr laments that he has become a villain in the story where he finds himself, a story that is history and, as such, will end up in our history books. Unlike the founding fathers, Frankenstein's creature is not concerned with his legacy. Speaking to Walton over his creator's remains, he explains, "when I die, I am well satisfied that abhorrence and opprobrium should load my memory . . . vice has degraded me beneath the meanest animal."[8] The creature tells Walton what we well know: he didn't want to be a monster. "A frightful selfishness hurried me on, while my heart was poisoned with remorse . . . My heart was fashioned to be susceptible of love and sympathy; and, when wrenched by misery to vice and hatred, it did not endure the violence of the change without torture, such as you cannot even imagine."[9] Buried within this metaphor, we find a harvesting of hearts, a wrenching. Wrenched: twisted, turned, jerked, pulled, wrested out, pained, and so forth. Wretched.

In his influential essay "Monster Culture (Seven Theses)," Jeffrey Jerome Cohen concludes:

> Monsters are our children. They can be pushed to the farthest margins of geography and discourse, hidden away at the edges of the world and in the forbidden recesses of our mind, but they always return. And when they come back, they bring not just a fuller knowledge of our place in history and the history of knowing our place, but they bear self-knowledge, *human* knowledge—and a discourse all the more sacred as it arises from the Outside. These monsters ask us how we perceive the world, and how we have misrepresented what we have attempted to place. They ask us to reevaluate our cultural assumptions about race, gender, sexuality, our perception of difference, our tolerance toward its expression. They ask us why we have created them.[10]

I remember teaching the closing scenes of *Frankenstein* at Rutgers a few months after Hurricane Sandy, can see the faces and remember the astute comments of certain students as we discussed marginalization, not only the creature but also the window, the window through which he enters, to which he leaps when discovered by Walton, and through which he exits. It is the window and not the creature that is the monster, in this scene; the window is both the symbol and the structure of the creature's marginalization.

Earlier this week, Jeffrey Jerome Cohen—a Jew like me—self-published a short essay criticizing media coverage of the National Policy Institute meeting in Washington, D.C., where he is an English professor. Focusing on Nazi salutes in a ballroom where his son held his bar mitzvah celebration (and where his daughter will soon hold her bat mitzvah), Cohen highlights actions of resistance, refusal, and protest, suggesting that media coverage focused on hate-based "exuberance" rather than "other, more affirmative modes of passion." Ultimately, Cohen claims, "too many narratives marvel at the theatricality of hate . . . I want to be outside with the protesters."[11] This brings us back to the window—is the monster always outside it, on the margins, in the margin? Noting in his journal that a family of philosophical heavyweights "really does love me" while his own daughter raises her son—his namesake—across the ocean? (Mary Shelley named her first son William after her father even though they were all but estranged; Godwin's letters following William's death were famously unhelpful.)

There is an academic analysis to be written of the *Hamilton* protest; it is not mine to write. I know it has to do with the history of the theater as a public, and political, space; I know it has to do with the "leftish"-ness of *Hamilton* and its fans; I know it has to do with authority and manipulation. I do not know if the situation that led to the protest was staged with the protest in mind (pun not intended but credit taken for pun). I don't know how to play the cello. I don't know what my responsibilities are in relation to swastikas scribbled here and there, jotted down, public postscript, the John Hancock of hate.

Dear Theodosia, what to say to you?

Last night, my son was overtired, and I was feeding him some yogurt in bed (just a mattress on the floor, but still), already a bad idea, and my leg was stretched out to block a potential fall, also, clearly, a bad idea, and he toppled, and hit his head on the wooden crib in which he refuses to sleep, and he cried, and I called the nurse, and I let him watch too many cartoons, and I let him take off his pajamas, and he slept the whole night between us in just a diaper printed with skulls and crossbones, and when I could not sleep because he wanted to sleep with half of his body on my neck, I wondered about the connections between infancy and piracy, and between motherhood and piracy, and between cartoons and cognitive development, and between piracy and intellectual history.

In the second song of *Hamilton*, when Alexander Hamilton first meets Aaron Burr, when the play plays compare and contrast and we see how they foil each other, and we recognize what will turn out to be a deadly elective affinity, and I realize that my great-grandmother's bracelet, which says *sei gesund* (be well, take care, get real), has fallen off my wrist and worry it might be folded, an ironic choking hazard, somewhere in the folds of the cozy outfit you're wearing in an icy room where dolphins jump from cold, calm water and land on their sides, where dolphins cannot tell their histories of freedom and capture, Hamilton sings to Burr, *You're an orphan. Of course! I'm an orphan.* In a small book you own which is shaped like a dolphin and which I might be mixing up with a small book you own which is shaped like an elephant, a baby dolphin, speaking for baby dolphins everywhere, explains, *we love to play with our mothers.*[12] Accosted and befriended, Burr advises Hamilton, *talk less, smile more.*[13] In other words, act like a dolphin or a baby . . . *vice has degraded me beneath the meanest animal.* To harvest a heart is to be a pirate.

18

✦

Broken

On the final pages of *Frankenstein*, the creature explains himself to the explorer: "I, the miserable and the abandoned, am an abortion, to be spurned at, and kicked, and trampled on. Even now my blood boils at the recollection of this injustice . . . You hate me; but your abhorrence cannot equal that with which I regard myself. I look on the hands which executed the deed; I think on the heart in which the imagination of it was conceived, and long for the moment when they will meet my eyes, when it will haunt my thoughts, no more."[1]

Describing himself as an "abortion," the creature conflates his heart with his creator's heart. *The heart in which the imagination of it was conceived* refers at once to the creature's heart, in which the murderous plot was hatched, and to Frankenstein's heart, in which the creature, that is, the imagination and imaginer, the specter of the imaginary and the plotter of plot twists, was conceived. In this case, to be conceived is to be aborted.

Only Barbara Johnson could slide from P. B. Shelley's "Ode to the West Wind" to twentieth-century debates about abortion in America. She does this via the flash-bulb illumination of apostrophe: "Because of the ineradicable tendency of language to animate whatever it addresses, rhetoric itself can always have already answered 'yes' to the question of whether a fetus is a human being."[2] To talk to something, even if it's not there (he's not there, she's not there), is to render something "animated, anthropomorphized, 'person-ified.' "[3] This is true not only of the fetus but also of literature, or, rather, of literary figures. If the author is dead then literary criticism brings her back to life. And Johnson writes, "the undecidable *is* the political. There is politics precisely because there is undecidability."[4] Debates about Mary Shelley—her commitments, her impulses, her legacy—as well as arguments for her enduring value and for her canonicity, lend her a political charge. *Frankenstein* is thus rendered a feminist touchstone. At least for me, who became a Romanticist before I became a mother and before I fully understood that I was a feminist.

Beyond poems and legal tractates on the topic of abortion, Johnson posits, "there may be a deeper link between motherhood and apostrophe than we have hitherto suspected":

> If demand is the originary vocative, which assures life even as it inaugurates alienation, then it is not surprising that questions of animation inhere in the rhetorical figure of apostrophe. The reversal of apostrophe we noted in the Shelley poem ("animate me") would be no reversal at all, but a reinstatement of the primal apostrophe in which, despite Lacan's disclaimer, there is precisely a link between demand and animation, between apostrophe and life-and-death dependency. If apostrophe is structured like demand, and if demand articulates the primal relation to the mother as a relation to the Other, then lyric poetry itself—summed up in the figure of apostrophe—comes to look like the fantastically intricate history of endless elaborations and displacements of the single cry, "Mama!"[5]

Now, I have complex feelings about that L-word, "lyric." But I'm a mom now, and I don't need apostrophe and/or lyric theory and/or P. B. Shelley to show me that all language and all literature derives from a cry for mama.

Frankenstein's creature cries *mama* a lot; Frankenstein doesn't listen. He promises to make the creature a mate, but breaks that promise via an abortion. He takes a trip with his BFF Henry (with whom you know I think he is in love), planning to "fulfil my promise while abroad," hoping to return "a free man."[6] He takes his damn time, winding through England, the moody antihero of a Wes Anderson movie, "haunted by a curse that shut up every avenue to enjoyment" despite the castles, ravines, etc.[7] He sees "an insurmountable barrier placed between me and my fellow-men; this barrier was sealed with the blood of William and Justine," the creature's first victims.[8] A few days before my water broke, I lost the mucus plug, which is the most disgusting compound noun but really filled me with the thrill of fearful excitement. We took my birth bag, took a trial run at the hospital. The nurse, Laura, smelled thickly of hairspray, checked my cervix, hooked me up to the fetal monitors, sent me home a few hours later. I met her again when my son came—she was the second of three delivery nurses whose shifts I labored through, she held me still while I wailed and the needle was inserted in my back. The doctors were all too respectful; Laura's the one who finally said, *get an epidural and go to sleep*. She saved me. She clocked out right when I started pushing and it still kind of bothers me that she didn't meet my son. What must it be like to be Laura and to spend one's working hours immersed in that kind of intimacy?

In literary history, *Laura* is an ideal woman; we get this from Petrarch. My favorite professor of early modern literature pronounced it Low-ra, the sound I moaned, curled up on the bed, your father's arms around me, *Parks and Recreation* playing on his laptop. (In the nights following the election, I played it when I couldn't sleep, my fast-food feminism.)

Petrarch only ever shows us his Laura in bits and pieces. Nancy J. Vickers aligns his piecemeal construction of beauty with dismemberment. She writes, "Laura is always presented as a part or parts of a woman. When more than one part figures in a single poem, a sequential, inclusive ordering is never stressed. Her textures are those of metals and stones; her image is that of a collection of exquisitely beautiful disassociated objects."[9] This is not only "bodily disintegration" and "descriptive dismemberment" but also the memory of how one sees one's mother.[10] My necklace, for example, which my mother gave me for Valentine's Day when I was eighteen, a small, bright heart. You play with it often; you swatted your little friend's hand away when she tried to touch it. *Mine*. Last night, as I cradled you and read you stories accompanied by a rabbit puppet, you pinched it and then tried, insistently, to pinch a dark freckle, a spot on my upper breast, a breast on which you have slept since your first day in this world without ever having spotted this mark or wondered at its signification or tried to take it off of me, to take me apart.

You recently learned the word *button* and now you point to the freckles on my face saying *butt, butt, butt*.

Vickers reads Petrarch with Ovid and with beauty to show us what changes under pressure and why. This provides a definition of poetry: "For it is in fact the loss, at the fictional level, of Laura's body that constitutes the intolerable absence, creates a reason to speak, and permits a poetic 'corpus' . . . Laura and *lauro*, the laurel to crown a poet laureate, are one."[11]

Frankenstein hides himself away in a desolate Scottish cottage; Frankenstein gets to work. "In this retreat I devoted the morning to labour; but in the evening, when the weather permitted, I walked on the stony beach of the sea, to listen to the waves as they roared, and dashed at my feet."[12] In contrast to "the roarings of the giant ocean," Frankenstein remembers the "fair lakes" of Switzerland as "the play of a lively infant."[13] Frankenstein proceeds in his "labour," getting ready for the birth, despite his disgust at his work. He explains, "During my first experiment, a kind of enthusiastic frenzy had blinded me to the horror of my employment; my mind was intently fixed on the sequel of my labour, and my eyes were shut to the horror of my proceedings. But now I went to it in cold blood, and my heart often sickened at the work of my hands"; his "forebodings of evil . . . made my heart sicken in my bosom."[14] Frankenstein labors "in cold blood"; by aborting his project, he dooms his original creation to be an "abortion" with blood that "boils."

This is no blazon. Hell, this is not even a poem. Frankenstein starts to freak out. Maybe this new creature won't like her intended mate, or will be cruel and murderous. Perhaps "one of the first results of those sympathies for which the daemon thirsted would be children, and a race of devils would be propagated upon the earth."[15]

The monster's at the threshold, watching, waiting. Frankenstein's "heart failed within [him]," and one glance at the creature's face, the ugliness of which implies badness, is enough to make him break his promise:

> As I looked on him, his countenance expressed the utmost extent of malice and treachery. I thought with a sensation of madness on my promise of creating another like to him, and, trembling with passion, tore to pieces the thing on which I was engaged. The wretch saw me destroy the creature on whose future existence he depended for happiness, and, with a howl of devilish despair and revenge, withdrew.[16]

My students always wonder at the cruelty of this moment. Why rip the mate to shreds? It's not as though anybody else has the power to animate her. Why "tremble with passion"; why "destroy" in this way? Why this conflation of violence and refusal?

It's not uncommon for my students to read this as a sexual assault, a murder, a criminal provocation. It is at least also a scene of birth—of Frankenstein as monster, of the creature as irredeemably, definitely monstrous. It is a birth and it is also an abortion. But what of its scattering, and what of beauty? In an essay connecting art vandalism and disability studies, Tobin Siebers writes:

The act of vandalism changes the referential function of the art work, creating a new image in its own right. If this is true, two unforeseen consequences present themselves. First, the act of vandalism is an act of creation because a new image comes to life. Second, if a new image is created, it is potentially the case that a new referent also emerges.[17]

By ripping the creature's mate-in-process to pieces on the cold cottage floor, Frankenstein writes the remainder of his story. He tells his enraged creature, "The hour of my weakness is past, and the period of your power is arrived."[18] In other words, the creature has the power, but his creator has the control. To create another like him and let them loose would have been to relinquish that control. By contrast, the creature has "a smothered voice" and "the impotence of anger."[19] To be a monster is to be "the slave, not the master of an impulse, which I detested, yet could not disobey," as the creature eventually explains to Walton.[20] Cf. Roland Barthes: "the birth of the reader must be at the cost of the death of the Author."[21] Your monster's only a monster when you become a monster, yourself.

And what of the female body, the destruction of which leads to this monstrous twin birth? Frankenstein explains that he placed the "relics of [his] work . . . into a basket, with a great quantity of stones, and laying them up, determined to throw them into the sea that very night."[22] Frankenstein takes care of these "relics," these holy parts of the monstrous whole, in the wee hours:

> Between two and three in the morning the moon rose; and I then, putting my basket aboard a little skiff, sailed out about four miles from the shore. The scene was perfectly solitary: a few boats were returning towards land, but I sailed away from them. I felt as if I was about the commission of a dreadful crime, and avoided with shuddering anxiety any encounter with my fellow-creatures. At one time the moon, which had before been clear, was suddenly overspread by a thick cloud, and I took advantage of the moment of darkness, and cast my basket into the sea; I listened to the gurgling sound as it sunk, and then sailed away from the spot. The sky became clouded; but the air was pure, although chilled by the north-east breeze that was then rising. But it refreshed me, and filled me with such agreeable sensations, that I resolved to prolong my stay on the water, and fixing the rudder in a direct position, stretched myself at the bottom of the boat.[23]

Petrarchan, but darker, Frankenstein's scattering of the body in the water. She gurgles as she goes down and he feels damn good. Following Siebers, we might ask what referent emerges when this new image submerges. Frankenstein's all but gotten out of ever having sex with Elizabeth (to point out his resistance and delay to such intimacy represents a consummately unoriginal observation). He's also secured the creature's current and future monstrosity, thereby skipping out on any potential parental obligation. Breaking and sinking his promise leaves Frankenstein perfectly alone—he's alone, which is perfect. At the scene of abortion, it's his living child, the one to whom he owes at least the promise of companionship, the one to whom he speaks with animating, vivifying language, who is aborted. It is not the aborting of the unborn but rather the spurning of the unwanted born that constitutes the monstrous act.

19

Taken

The friend who remembers the child I was reminds me, sometimes, who I was. Sleeping in a century-old mountain cabin, not quite pregnant, she observed I was *living the life I would have predicted when I was five*. When she met my husband, she told me I *would have picked him when I was fourteen and at summer camp*. Hiking, together, to the top of the third Flatiron, where the rocks are purple and the trees are bent and vision is cut away, we discussed becoming mothers. We took selfies with my dog, who seems intuitively to understand how selfies work. Perhaps I was pregnant already but did not realize it. A young buck, sick, followed us back, lolled in the yard, rested. The park ranger came, waited; eventually the deer summoned his strength, headed back up the mountain to who knows what fate.

My friend is a doula and will soon be a midwife. The midwife who helped to bring Elena Adelaide Shelley into the world appears to have been named Gaetana Musto, but in general we know very little about that child.[1]

When we were younger and my friend lived in Italy she'd draw the most sublime scenes on her letters, a girl with an iPod on the train, a girl in a painting by the sea.

Friendships are powerful, even imperfect friendships. In her file on Elena Adelaide Shelley, Betty T. Bennett scrawls Mary Shelley's daughter's name beside Claire Clairmont's daughter's name (her daughter with Byron, her ill-fated, ill-begotten daughter). Bennett writes, *Allegra's full name = Clara Allegra Byron cf to Clara Everina Shelley—WHY?*[2] Charlotte Gordon suggests, "Mary named the baby Clara after her stepsister, signaling a change in the relationship" for the better;[3] this doesn't explain, however, why this stepsister, by then called Claire Clairmont, named her baby after herself.

We discussed our future children's names when we were still children (Susannah, Linnea). All of these imaginary children were girls. On the eighth day after I gave birth, you came over, and I introduced you (he was sleeping from trauma and sweet wine) and you said, *you've always loved that name.* This is true, but I do not know how you knew.

Arguably, Frankenstein's creature truly becomes a monster when he commits his first murder; the murder constitutes an aborted adoption. In a sense, what the creature does wrong is to try to adopt a beloved boy rather than an unwanted girl.

I have been thinking of unwanted girls. This is because my son and I have been listening to an audiobook version of *Anne of Green Gables*, which I am sure I would have loved but somehow missed as a girl. In the novel's opening chapters, Anne tells us, over and over, that nobody ever really wanted her, that no place has ever really been home.

Everybody wanted Elena, or, perhaps, everyone wanted to hide the fact that nobody wanted Elena. That's part of the reason we know so little about her. In a review of James Bieri's Percy Shelley biography, Matthew Borushko explains that one "must contend with Percy's, Mary's, and Claire's concerted effort to conceal the details of January and early February of 1819. Claire's journal is missing, Mary stopped her journal for those six weeks, and a depressed Percy would write to Peacock in England stating clearly for anyone else's eyes, 'we see absolutely no one here,' possibly concealing contact with someone connected to Elena Adelaide."[4] Despite these obfuscations and the limited details that remain, biographers have devised a system of theories. Bieri pursues the possibility that a fan of Queen Mab who followed the Shelleys across Europe might have conceived a child by Shelley.[5] Miranda Seymour favors the interpretation that Shelley adopted an abandoned child in a misguided attempt to comfort his wife, but that Mary rejected the child.[6] Charlotte Gordon argues that the Shelleys' nursemaid Elise might have conceived a child by Byron (possibly the result of a rape), and that the adoption of Elena Adelaide represents Mary Shelley's collaboration with her husband in support of a single mother with an illegitimate child.[7] These divergent accounts not only make different use of biographical details but also differ in their feminist commitments.

There has been much discussion of Elena Adelaide's genesis but what of Elena Adelaide herself? We know only that she was born, was registered, was named, was baptized, was left behind in Naples, and died. Some days I cannot help but linger in the aching maternal space carved out by the many short lives of Elena Adelaide Shelley. I refuse to formulate my own theory in part because I wish to protect her. To know her story would be to lose all other possibilities.

Frankenstein's creature also attempts an adoption that ends in death. Spurned, rejected, and turned out, he heads to Geneva and lies down in a field for a "slight sleep."[8] The creature recounts that this sleep "was disturbed by the approach of a beautiful child, who came running into the recess I had chosen with all the sportiveness of infancy."[9] It's a fascinating conjunction, that "with." William, Victor Frankenstein's beautiful baby brother (and, in name at least, Mary Shelley's beautiful son), comes running "with all the sportiveness of infancy." But a little syntactic pressure reveals that the creature had also "chosen" his "recess . . . with all the sportiveness of infancy."

It must be an appealing spot, this "hiding-place among the fields that surround it."[10] Indeed, to children (and to childlike creatures), there's something irresistible about a good hiding place. With the friend who reminds me of the child I was, I'd ride a bike so many times around the driveway it seemed we must be lost; we'd then couch ourselves in the low and lazy arms of a large pine. We'd meet at morning recess in the mossy place behind two stones. There was even a cave in the mountains just beyond her house to which we'd climb, in which we'd hide. Once, a bit older, we built clay aliens, brought them to the cave and to an adjoining cliff, and staged an earth landing.

Elena Adelaide is not the only child in the margins of Mary Shelley's life. While she was pregnant with Clara Everina and finishing *Frankenstein*, Percy Shelley "talked Mary into taking in a village girl, Polly Rose, whose family was too poor to provide for her."[11] When Percy Shelley abandoned Harriet to elope with Mary, he also left behind a daughter, Ianthe, and a son in utero, who would be named Charles. When Harriet, again pregnant, drowned herself, the courts refused to hand these children over to their radical, atheist, countercultural father. Gordon writes that this was "an extremely unusual ruling in the nineteenth century, when a father's rights were rarely questioned. There was no appeal process, no fighting the decision. Shelley's friends managed to appoint a clergyman to talk him out of his wild kidnapping plans."[12] Is it any wonder there are so many biographies of the Shelley circle?

Mary Shelley's niece, Clara Allegra (Alba) Byron, was also born in the nineteenth century. For this reason, Mary Shelley's stepsister, Claire, had no real claim on her. This might be why she named the child, in some small way, after herself. (The child's original name and then nickname, Alba, was a nod to Byron. In the unpublished biography, Bennett calls Allegra's full name "a permanent reminder to the child and the father of the mother's identity."[13]) Like Clara Everina and, presumably, Elena Adelaide, Allegra was a child. And like William Frankenstein, the creature is a child. So there must be some connection between hiding and holding.

Faced with young William, "an idea seized" the creature, "that this little creature was unprejudiced, and had lived too short a time to have imbibed a horror of deformity." This creature, the creature muses, might go with him and be his companion and friend, so that he will "not be so desolate in this peopled earth." But kids are cruel—kids are, possibly, the cruelest, and William screams, and he calls the creature a "hideous monster," an "ugly wretch," an "ogre." William thinks he is in a fairy tale and in a sense he is, but fairy tales are often really horror stories.

One pities little William. Imagine finding a childhood hiding place only to be seized and told that you will "never see your father again," the imaginative space of cozy isolation rendered, suddenly, real.

We know how this story ends. William reveals his parentage; the creature utters, "you shall be my first victim":

> The child still struggled, and loaded me with epithets which carried despair to my heart: I grasped his throat to silence him, and in a moment he lay dead at my feet.
> I gazed on my victim, and my heart swelled with exultation and hellish triumph: clapping my hands, I exclaimed, "I, too, can create desolation; my enemy is not impregnable . . ."[14]

Etymologically speaking, impregnable—invincible—is probably not linked to pregnancy, but instead represents a corruption of the French *prenable*, "able to be taken." Even so, here, it suggests *impregnate*, and aligns pregnancy with vulnerability and with its (negated) opposite. Silencing is strangulation; the heart of the monster (now, surely, he has followed suit and become a monster) turns from "despair" to "hellish triumph" at this transmutation.

Do we need to talk about Justine?

Frankenstein is the story of how we make our own monsters; thus it is a story for every age. Today, I am reading *Frankenstein* as a cautionary tale about the monstrosity of silence.

William's wearing a small portrait of his mother—it's attractive to the monster—but then reminds him that he'll never have a lover—he's read enough to know how to screw someone over—he places it in the folds of Justine's dress—Justine, who just happens to be a beloved friend and servant of the Frankenstein family—she's accused of the murder, forced to confess, and executed—Victor Frankenstein watches it all happen and says nothing—following many bad excuses that mostly add up to the argument that nobody would believe him, anyway. Drawing on Carl Jung in a paper she wrote on *Frankenstein* during her freshman year of college, my friend wrote, *If the shadow is not assimilated, it will find a way to bring itself into life.*

Unlike or like Elena Adelaide, Justine is a young girl marked by the cruelty of her mother ("This girl had always been the favourite of her [dead] father; but, through a strange perversity, her mother could not endure her").[15] The monster means to punish Justine for representing pretty girls everywhere, who, he has learned, would reject him; ironically, he ends up murdering a being not unlike himself.

Sometimes I indulge myself and wonder what would have happened if Frankenstein's creature had stumbled upon Mathilda's cottage. Bear with me, here. Would a beautiful girl who thought herself to be a monster see the monster's crushed beauty? Would she provide him with a portion of food, as she might a fox? As a fox might, might he suffer her to pat his head?

I'm in your book? Laughs the friend who reminds me of the child I was. I'm standing in the bathroom, her face framed by the edges of my phone. She can't see me, is looking, instead, at my son, who is fresh from the bathtub and holding his toothbrush.

Are you brushing your teeth? my friend asks.

What? my son replies, exuberantly.

20

✦

Will

On cold afternoons, my son taps a page with crayons, affixes, with difficulty, the dog sticker. The first time he got one to lay flat, he shouted *I did it!* He had not said this before, and has not said it since. This is the way his language comes, in fits and starts, the times he speaks without thinking and the times he thinks he is speaking, but is not. Of a Sabbath afternoon, the large piece of challah he considers, carefully, and then raises up, proclaiming, *wallet.*

It isn't that children don't leave archives but they don't leave the archives we know.

There's a moment in Mary Shelley's journal when she writes:

> —in the evening Willy
> falls
> out of bed, & is not hurt[1]

and it reads like a William Carlos Williams poem, the word falls falling to the next line, the eye following him down and out of bed.

Just shy of the one-month anniversary of William Shelley's death, Mary Shelley's journal imagines an act of grand erasure: "We have now lived ~~now~~ five years together & if all the events of the five years were blotted out I might be happy—but to have won & then cruelly have lost the associations of four years is not an accident ~~that~~ to which the human mind can bend ~~to~~ without much suffering."[2] And there is so much we can say and so much that has been said about that erasure, how she lived it, and wept, and who was kind, and who was cruel, and whether they meant to be kind, and were cruel, anyway, by accident. But I am trying to find William, to hold him for a moment in my mind, not his absence but his presence.

In a letter written to her husband when William was about one year and eight months old, Mary Shelley offers a theory of elective affinities:

> The behaviour of this child to the two little girls [his sister Clara and cousin Allegra/"Alba"] would be an argument in favour of those who advocate <u>instinctive natural affection</u> He will not go near Alba and if she approaches him he utters a fretful cry until she is removed—but he kisses Clara—strokes her arms & feet and laughs to find them so soft and pretty and the other day when he got a twig of mignionet after he had smelt it and handed it all round he put it to her nose to scent.[3]

Later, in Rome, where he will die, Mary Shelley writes, "We took our Will-man to the Vatican & he was delighted with the Goats & the Cavalli and dolefully lamented over the <u>man rotto</u> which is his kind of language." If, as Bennett surmises in her notes, the "man rotto" indicates broken statues, then with the juxtaposition of these images we perceive the confluence of sweetness and gore that makes little boys so delicious. When she wrote letters about William and the "men rotti," Mary Shelley was already pregnant with her second son, the one who would survive.[4]

Of these "men rotti"—these broken men—art history and aesthetic theory have much to say. First, there's the Romantic obsession with fragments and ruins, with broken antiquities and crumbling cathedrals and poems unfinished on purpose. Describing his sublime mindscape after seeing the Elgin Marbles, which are essentially pieces of a holy temple England stole, Keats concludes with a famous phrase: *a shadow of a magnitude.*[5] This is not a bad description of Willy's archive, his mother's fond mentions jotted down, what little we know of what she lost. Charlotte Gordon tells us that, shortly before his death, "Wilmouse [a nickname] thrilled [Percy] Shelley by saying 'Father.' "[6]

The first graders were having recess on our neighborhood playground this morning, and a cluster of girls took a special interest in us. *I wish this little boy were my baby brother-sister,* one said wistfully. *What is he trying to say?* they questioned me, as my son shouted, *Hi! Whoa!* When they realized I wasn't going to hand over my baby for them to play with, the girls rolled up a winter coat, named her Jay-Jay, and pushed her in the swing beside us. *How old is your baby?* asked Jayla, Jay-Jay's mother. *One,* I replied. *How old is your baby? Two,* Jayla answered. *Almost two,* corrected Sloane, who was pretending to be Jay-Jay's big sister. *Two and a half*, Jayla chimed back in. *She's not* straight *two*. My son was fascinated, the purple coat doted on, pushed, swung beside him. I explained the game to him. *Does he understand what you're saying? Does he understand what you're telling him?* In truth, I didn't know. *He understands more than he can say*, I offered. Barbara Johnson writes that mothers affix words to the world for us, as "a child comes into language through the mother's address."[7]

And what did William Shelley understand? The broken sculptures were "his language." Rilke tells us of an archaic torso: "there is no place / that does not see you. You must change your life."[8] (Drafting his poem on William's death, Percy Shelley referred to his son as a "ruined creature," then crossed that phrase out.[9])

Mary Shelley wasn't having it. In a letter from Rome to Maria Gisborne, she writes:

> The place is full of English, rich, noble—important and foolish. I am sick of it—I am sick of seeing the world in dumb show, and but that I am in Rome, in the city where stocks and stones defeat a million of times over my father's quoted maxim, "that a man is better than a stock or a stone," who could see the Apollo, and a Dandy spying at it, and not be of my opinion—Our little Will is delighted with the goats and the horses and the men rotti, and the ladie's [*sic*] white marbel [*sic*] feet.[10]

Here, Mary Shelley casts the Romantic aesthetics of the fragmented and ruined as child's play, as a fascinating object for snobby, childish tourists—or for children themselves. The language of the broken man isn't deep and transcendent and sublime. It doesn't glow from within, or whatever Rilke said. It's brutal, the language of a little boy. Violence inheres in what's missing.

Yesterday, my son crashed his entire skull into my nose, seemed surprised when I yelped, then leaned in and offered a feel-better kiss.

A few weeks before William's death, the three-year-old sat for a portrait. The artist was Amelia Curran, a family friend who lived in Rome. Gordon paints the scene:

Mary did not want [William] in an artificial pose, so instead of buttoning him into dress clothes, she allowed him to wear his nightshirt. Amelia put a rose in his hand and William let the shirt slide down his shoulder, chattering happily in both Italian and English while Amelia worked at her easel. During the first few days, she made good progress. She captured the little boy's pointed chin and delicate features. A wisp of hair brushes his forehead. His arms are plump and dimpled. He looks past the painter, intent, as though he is listening to someone—his mother, his aunt Claire, or his father, perhaps.

But a few days into the project, the little boy began to feel sick.[11]

Things went quickly after that. A stomachache, diagnosis of worms, the onset of malaria, sometimes called "Roman fever."[12]

Back up a moment, please. Gordon writes that he "looks past the painter." And this, indeed, is how he looks at you—the way that other people's children look at you.

The nightdress falling off his shoulder reveals his nipple; you could be forgiven for mistaking this for a mother's portrait, the rose blooming, welcoming, the pink lips, the bud suggesting something evermore about to be.

It seems likely that Curran completed the portrait after the child's death, which could explain the darkened background, the halo of green-blue light around his head suggesting a sort of radioactive, monstrous glow. I am not an art historian but I imagine there was scenery behind him that Amelia Curran blotted out or swirled together, for he was no longer in the world.

In the portrait, William Shelley looks at you. He says *hi*. He says *whoa*.

21

Brevity

after Anne Carson

On December 27, 1818, either a child was born in Naples or she was not.

If a child was born in Naples, either she was named Elena Adelaide Shelley or she was not.

If the child was named Elena Adelaide Shelley, either Percy Bysshe Shelley was her father or he adopted her.

If he adopted her, either he did so to placate Mary Shelley's ravenous grief or he did so for some other reason.

If he adopted her to placate Mary Shelley's ravenous grief, then either he was successful or he was not.

If Percy Bysshe Shelley was the child's father, he may have claimed that Mary Shelley was the mother but she was not.

If he adopted the child for some other reason, then either it was Mary Shelley's idea or it was not.

If Percy Bysshe Shelley was the child's father, then the mother could have been Mary's stepsister or a servant or a reader or someone else entirely or maybe not.

If Elena Adelaide Shelley was teething or just fussy. If Elena Adelaide Shelley was smiling or just gassy. If Elena Adelaide Shelley was what is sometimes called *a good sleeper*.

Either Mary Shelley knew who the mother was or she did not.

After Elena Adelaide was born, either Mary Shelley held her or she did not.

If Mary Shelley held Elena Adelaide, either this holding was ordinary or it was not.

After the Shelleys left Naples, either Elena Adelaide was lonely or she was not.

When Elena Adelaide died, aged one year five months and fourteen days, either Mary Shelley wept or she did not.

Clarity

Like any good mother, Betty T. Bennett went looking for "little Clara." Apparently, in Italy, the girl was called *Chiara*, an Italian name that I have always liked, because it is perfect. Brightness and lightness, sweetness and light, a very small body in the ground.

In a series of emails to a colleague on sabbatical in Venice, Bennett writes: *I think at this point, the most important thing is to try to locate little Clara Shelley's burial site. Then, perhaps for the rest, basta???* And: *I hope we will be able to figure out where Clara Everina Shelley, who was only one year old and died on 24 September 1818 at Venice, is buried. So far, all I have found is that she is buried on the Lido . . .* And: *it turns out no one has ever looked for records or the cemetery where the child is buried and I think it would add greatly to the biography . . .*[1]

My Clara, that is, my great-grandmother, carried two long, brass candlesticks to America, candlesticks to kindle the Sabbath in her new home. Once, my father (her grandson) sent her a book and wrapped it so carefully she could not open it. Last week, her bracelet fell off my wrist in the city.

In her *Introduction* to Mary Shelley, Bennett writes:

> It is always difficult to understand the tides of relationships from an observer's perspective—and even from a participant's. But certainly two closely linked tragedies threatened the Shelleys' union. On 24 September 1818 one-year-old Clara Everina Shelley died of dysentery at Venice. The Shelleys were bereft. Then, on 7 June 1819 William Shelley, almost three and a half, succumbed to malaria. The devastated Mary Shelley wrote, "I never know one moments ease from the wretchedness & despair that possesses me—May you my dear

Marianne never know what it is to lose two only & lovely children
in one year—to watch their dying moments—& then at last to be left
childless & for ever miserable."

Both Shelleys deeply mourned their loss, but for Mary Shelley the
deaths of their children seemed an insurmountable grief. Just as in
1816, when she half-apologetically teased P. B. Shelley about want-
ing another baby, she makes clear over and again in her letters and
journals that she was not the unwilling sexual and maternal partner
she has sometimes been made out to be, that her children were crucial
to her life. She writes that she "ought to have died on the 7th of June
last" (William's death) and goes so far as to say she would rather
have forgone her years with P. B. Shelley than "cruelly have lost the
associations of four years."[2]

But why go looking for "little Clara's" burial site? What could it possibly
add to this biography?

In a letter announcing William's death, Frankenstein's father writes, "William is dead!—that sweet child, whose smiles delighted and warmed my
heart, who was so gentle, yet so gay! . . . I will not attempt to console
you . . . Your dear mother! Alas, Victor! I now say, Thank God she did
not live to witness the cruel, miserable death of her youngest darling!"[3]
Upon learning the news, Henry admits, "I can offer you no consolation";
in lieu of "common topics of consolation," he tells his friend that William
"does not now feel the murderer's grasp; a sod covers his gentle form,
and he knows no pain."[4] But can this sod itself, or finding the sod, offer
some form of consolation, communication, or even understanding? Having remained silent throughout Justine's trial, conviction, and execution,
Frankenstein tells us, "Justine died; she rested; and I was alive."[5]

Betty Bennett's email correspondence with her colleague in Venice raises
the possibility that Clara/Chiara might have been buried in a Jewish cemetery. This colleague—Romeo Segnan, a physics professor on
sabbatical—writes: "The Lido has a Jewish cemetery and I have some
information on it, including the fact that Lord Byron began his horse-
back riding trips from the cemetery and would proceed along the beach.
Apparently Shelley accompanied him on these rides. They all knew about
the cemetery and it could be that Mary Shelley was allowed to bury her
baby there." Bennett responds, "My friend . . . tells me that there had
been a Protestant cemetery up until 1810 at San Nicolo al Lido. The Jewish cemetery nearby was granted land in 1386. He says after 1810 the

Protestant cemetery was no longer in operation, and it was removed with construction of the airport in the 1930s. Since the Shelleys [*sic*] daughter died in 1818, there may well be a chance she is buried in the Jewish cemetery."

But she couldn't have been buried in the Jewish cemetery, I tell my husband, and he says that I am putting too much weight on distinctions. He says, *a separation could be made with just a piece of string.*

Following the visit, Romeo Segnan writes, "we also enjoyed your visit. It was interesting and fun to search the Archives and the Hebrew Cemetery at the Lido"; letters and emails from the following year, however, indicate that the search was unsuccessful.

Picture this: the scholar in large part responsible for Mary Shelley's canonicity and for our understanding of her complexity weaving her way through a Jewish cemetery looking for a lost child. A scholar who identified with Mary Shelley as a wife, widow, and mother, and who devoted her career to another woman's legacy, touching, lightly, but lightly, the crumbling graves, their Hebrew letters, looking for Mary Shelley's daughter among the bodies of the Jews, bodies that, given the very little I know about wet, sweet Venice and what I know of Jewish burial, its thin clothes and simple wood, must have crumbled quickly away.

Betty Bennett found clarity. At least, that's what the draft of her unfinished book—the capacious Mary Shelley biography on which she was working when she died—suggests. Bennett writes:

> Clara Shelley was buried in the burial ground for foreigners within the Forte de San Nicolo. An Austrian fortress at the north end of the Lido, this bastion was the only cemetery in which non-Catholics were supposed to be buried in Venice, though the Lido contained an operative Jewish cemetery.
>
> In the journal, Mary Shelley noted simply on 26 and 27 September, "Go to Lido" . . . No mention of Clara's grave, but in her 1823 poem, <u>The Choice</u>, she recalled how "my sweet girl,/ whose face resembled <u>his</u>, / Slept on bleak Lido, near Venetian seas."[6]

I wonder who will edit this biography, will do for Bennett what she did for Shelley. In "The Heads of the Town Up to the Aether," Jack Spicer writes, "Imagine this as lyric poetry."[7] Sitting among crayons and lipsticks while my son and his father share their usual Sabbath nap, I write, *imagine this as feminism.*

The last time we see the monster, he's headed out the "cabin-window" and toward "the most northern extremity of the globe." He tells Walton, "Neither yours nor any man's death is needed to consummate the series of my being, and accomplish that which must be done; but it requires my own." By describing his death as the death of "no man," Frankenstein's creation portrays himself not only as a nonhuman monster but also as a woman; like a woman, he promises to take care of what must be done. This, he tells us, will be his death by sacrificial burning, destroying, at once, monster, memory, and artifact. (For some reason, in her file on William and Clara Shelley, Betty T. Bennett has a handwritten definition of the word "artifact.") Like William Frankenstein, at least according to Henry, the creature tells us that, in death, he "shall no longer feel the agonies which now consume [him]"; death, at this point, is his "only consolation." Before he springs from the window, the creature comforts us: "I shall die, and what I now feel be no longer felt."[8]

23

✦

Fox's Heart

Just as Diana was "the life of [Mathilda's father's] life," his "memory" is "the life of [her] life."[1] The novella's dénouement is slick and swift and painful. Mathilda reads her father's letter, realizes he's suicidal, chases or follows or drives him to the sea, arrives too late. (Following her husband's death by drowning, Mary Shelley would refer to this scene as if it were a prophecy.[2]) En route to the ocean, our shy girl becomes witchy. The "fever of [her] blood became intolerable." She tells a servant that her father is only dead if the next lightning strike hits a particular tree; it hits the tree. (In seminar, poet Jessica Comola called this Mathilda's *supernatural logic*.) Delirious, she's plunged into visions from the previous night's nightmares.

> My garments were wet and clung around me, and my hair hung in straight locks on my neck when not blown aside by the wind. I shivered, yet my pulse was high with fever . . . my eyes wild and inflamed were starting from my head.

When it becomes clear that things aren't going to end well, a piece of her dies. "My heart no longer beat wildly; I did not feel any fever: but I was chilled; my knees sunk under me—I almost slept as I walked with excess of weariness; every limb trembled." Looking back, she reflects that "the cold rain that fell about my heart . . . has changed it to stone."[3] Life among people with her secret feels like an ongoing deceit (in this context, she has a "dove's look and fox's heart"); she fakes her death; she retires to a "wide solitude," a simple life in nature with occasional visits from a servant and, eventually, a poet friend. While she specifies that she "would not remain on the sea coast, but proceeded immediately inland," my students imagined Mathilda by the shore, or underwater: she experiences the "gentle current" of her "feelings"; her view is "bounded only by the horizon"; she fixes herself on solitude as on a guiding star. Mathilda tells us that "a fox came every day for a portion of food appropriated for him and would suffer me to pat his head"; thus she situates herself in a tenuous, simple relationship with her own wild heart. She becomes, she tells us, "a selfish solitary creature."[4]

Even so, she "wished for one heart in which I could pour unrestrained my plaints"; she finds this in the poet Woodville, who has lost his lover. Mathilda explains that his "misfortunes . . . were not of the heart's core like mine," and tells us we may "judge how cold [her] heart must have been not to be warmed" by him. The loss of Woodville's bride to illness "was a natural grief, not to destroy but to purify the heart"; "His heart was simple like a child." Recounting Woodville's story, Mathilda tells us that he "was enraptured in possessing the heart" of his lover, that, as her death approached, "His heart, he knew not why, prognosticated misfortune"; following the tragedy, he wanted to "converse only with his own heart."[5] She calls his heart "worldly"; she calls it "whole."[6]

By contrast, Mathilda's heart and blood continue to pollute her narrow frame. She writes, "unlawful and detestable passion had poured its poison into my ears and changed all my blood, so that it was no longer the kindly stream that supports life but a cold fountain of bitterness corrupted in its very source." She feels "polluted"; she calls herself a "monster." Woodville affirms this sense when he tells her, "your pulses beat and you breathe, yet you seem already to belong to another world."[7] The closest we get to a sex scene between these two is the joint suicide Mathilda proposes, a twisted version of seduction and repulsion, her broken heart and his heartening words.

Such has been her education.

Indeed I dare not die. I have a mother whose support and hope I am.

Having killed her mother in childbirth, having lost three children, having lived through her half-sister's suicide and her husband's pregnant then-wife's suicide, and likely experiencing at least some degree of prenatal anxiety (hormones, common sense), it seems very likely that Mary Shelley might have feared, or even assumed, on her darker days, on the days she wrote *Mathilda*, that either she or the child inside her would soon die.

Even today, I had to sign a waiver saying *I understand*. I understand that you might need to remove my child from my body with a vacuum, with forceps, with scissors, with a knife. I understand that one or both of us could die. There is no more poetic way to say this.

A little patience, and all will be over[8]—at the moment of seduction, these family, deathbed words, handed down like an empty locket, a scratched strand of pearls, one lace glove.

"In love with death" and feeling it "to be near at hand," Mathilda sums up the "different scenes of [her] short life." She recalls, "Almost from infancy I was deprived of all the testimonies of affection which children generally receive . . . my father returned and I could pour my warm affections on a human heart."[9]

Mathilda tells Woodville, by which I mean, Mary Shelley tells Percy Florence: "you are the sole tie that binds me to existence . . . shed a few natural tears due to my memory . . . your heart is the only tomb in which my memory will be interred." *Don't wish that you had seen me die*, for "it is one of those adversities which hurt instead of purifying the heart."[10]

"So day by day I become weaker, and life flickers in my wasting form, as a lamp about to lose its vivifying oil."[11] Read in the context of *Mathilda*, we see our tragic heroine's life flicker away. But there is another context—life flickers, vivified by her life. But there is other oil.

Mathilda's incantation, driving toward the sea: "Alive! Alive!"[12]

That feeling I never fully understood until I became a mother: *if it has to be one of us, then please, let it be me.*

A mother, like an ark, is a clumsy kind of machine. It gets you through the deluge.

24

Lost

It is possible that Clara Shelley (February 22, 1815–March 6, 1815) was conceived on Mary Wollstonecraft's grave. It is possible that Byron would have forgotten to claim his daughter with Mary Shelley's stepsister, Clara Allegra (Alba) Byron (January 12, 1817–April 19, 1822), had he not been reminded by Percy Shelley. It is possible that Percy Shelley would not have reminded Byron if Mary had not reminded him.[1] If Mary hadn't reminded Shelley to remind Byron, perhaps the nursemaid, Elise, would not have traveled to Venice with Allegra. If Elise had not traveled to Venice with Allegra, she might not have written in a panic, and Percy might not have traveled to meet her and then sent for Mary, spurring a hasty trip with a sick child that precipitated the deaths of both Clara Everina Shelley (September 2, 1817–September 24, 1818) and William Shelley (January 24, 1816–June 7, 1819). Ultimately, Byron placed Allegra in a convent, where she died, too.

Of course, an infinite number of things are also possible.

To be a mother is to be the point of contact between a child and the world. I have worked hard to forget the importance of my actions. One cannot move when one thinks like this.

When Percy Bysshe Shelley eloped with Mary Shelley, he abandoned a young child and a pregnant wife. When that wife finally committed suicide, pregnant with a child that was possibly but probably not Shelley's, he failed to regain custody, and never saw those children again.

At some point, the Shelleys took in a village girl named Polly Rose. At another, they appear to have adopted an infant named Elena Adelaide.

Between her first daughter's death and the birth of Percy Florence Shelley (November 12, 1819–December 5, 1889), who was to be her only surviving child, Mary Wollstonecraft (Godwin) Shelley composed both *Frankenstein* and *Mathilda*, among other literary projects.

Stop it. An infinite number of things are also possible.

25

Afterbirth

In an age of transition, MWS's life and works represented human rights in transition.
—Betty T. Bennett, the unpublished biography

When Texas passed a bill requiring burial or cremation for fetal remains, a celebrated Victorianist wrote a series of tweets about her experiences with miscarriage. She imagined an alternate history in which she'd planned funeral after funeral on her way to becoming a mother. Either she deleted these tweets or I just can't find them.

A couple of weeks before her husband drowned, Mary Shelley suffered a near-fatal miscarriage:

> She haemorrhaged blood and slipped in and out of consciousness . . . [Shelley] forced Mary into an ice-filled bath, which at length stemmed the frightening flow of blood . . . She had lost a great deal of blood, had been convinced she was going to die, and for days afterwards was too weak to do more than crawl from her bed to the balcony overlooking the sea.[1]

The general consensus seems to be that Mary Shelley picked out Percy Florence's wife for him; she was a young widow (the wife, that is) and Mary felt, for her, an elective affinity.

I have been hearing, lately, that things are allowed to happen again when people forget. (You can't be an anti-vaxxer if you knew a kid with polio.)

Forgetting, then, is a form of becoming. But, as *Frankenstein* teaches us, creation is not always virtuous.

A couple months after my son was born, I called Anna, heard *this number has been disconnected* and stopped the stroller on the bridge, knowing. Anna did a lot of things: lived through the war in a school in Budapest, yelled at a man who threatened her sister in a public park (*I will be the one to call the police!*), worked in Jonas Salk's laboratory, translated several volumes of Einstein's letters and papers. When we shared a New Jersey neighborhood, she'd welcome me into a small house where Beethoven played, share with me her archive of poems and stories. When I called from Colorado to tell Anna I was pregnant, she asked, *what, with a baby?*

It was often hard for Anna to place a voice on the phone, a voice calling from another time. *But your voice is so peculiar . . .* The weight of the tragedy she'd lived through was so great, she could mention it dismissively, the way we forget about the effort it takes to pump the blood through our bodies. Eliding a story, the hand brushing aside, *when later my mother . . . was killed or whatever . . .*

In a commencement speech at Wellesley, citing the differences between *now* and *then*, which is to say, accounting for forgetting, Nora Ephron explained: "If you needed an abortion, you drove to a gas station in Union, New Jersey, with $500 in cash in an envelope and you were taken, blindfolded, to a motel room and operated on without an anesthetic."[2]

The legislation that might lead to a widespread abortion ban is often called "heartbeat" legislation. There are abortions in literature before and after Jemima's. I don't know why I thought its radicalism might adhere to its uniqueness. In that novel—which Mary Wollstonecraft was writing when she gave birth to Mary Shelley and died—Maria calls a mother "the only parent inclined to discharge a parent's duty."[3]

26

The Madre

The obituary for Sir Percy Florence Shelley (son of the poet) informs us that he died at his residence, aged 70. Though "he had been in bad health for some years . . . the fact was not generally known, as his indisposition had not confined him to the house." He *was* known as an "ardent tricyclist," was president of his rowing club, owned a steam yacht (*Oceana*) and ran an amateur theater out of his home. He and his wife had recently taken a "tour . . . down the west coast."[1]

In other words, things turned out pretty well.

This is the paradox of maternal anxiety, that one can only be certain in retrospect, and that one hopes for nothing more, yet hopes never to know.

I need to pause here to make space for the writing body. At present I sit at an antique desk, facing a bust of Percy Bysshe Shelley, which Leigh Hunt's wife, Marianne, modeled from memory fourteen years after his death. I am wearing Birkenstocks; they are having a high-fashion moment, but my overall appearance would not call this to mind. My leggings reveal a two-inch by one-inch patch of black hair on my left leg that I somehow keep missing, and that I have not had the presence of mind whilst shaving to conquer for several weeks. I am wearing a batik tunic that, while fashionable in its own right, is stained on the right breast by a redeye, which is a cup of coffee with an additional shot of espresso mixed in. And indeed my left eye is quite red, as my son, excitedly snuggling, kicked it very hard. His feet, which take after his father's, are exceptionally large for feet that have only been in the world for seven months.

I cannot decide whether to include the fact that this morning I gave myself a sponge bath using only baby wipes.

Yesterday, while I was looking at Percy Florence's collected letters to his step-aunt and mother's best frenemy, Claire Clairmont, my husband texted, *26th & Lex come quickly.*

On the way out the door, referring to Mary Shelley, I said, *I just don't know how she did it.*

The archivist smiled. *Servants? I mean, she had a nanny with her almost every step of the way.*

This is the mantra we throw at working mothers: *I don't know how she does it.*

One of my colleagues reported that a female graduate student had shown up at her office to discuss her hope of someday balancing a career in academia with the project of raising a family. On the phone after the meeting, my colleague was remorseful. *I said some shit about balance and priorities and working together, but the true answer to the question of how I do it all is money and processed food.*

On the occasion of his mother's death, Percy Florence's letters were minimal and devastated. In a famous passage, he writes, "You will have heard before this of the grievous calamity that has befallen me. I should have written before—but you will readily make allowances for me."[2] To Leigh Hunt, before insisting, protectively, that "I assure you I am quite unconscious of the irritability on the part of my mother that you allude to," he writes:

> I am sure that you will be much grieved to hear that my dear mother died last Saturday night. I will write by & bye [*sic*] and tell you more of it. I had intended writing to you before—but I have been unable to do so. and now you are one of very few that I have written to.[3]

There's so much certainty in these lines—certainty and pain. The letter is dated February 6, 1851. Exactly one year later, Percy Florence Shelley appeared in an amateur production of two plays performed at the theater on his estate. In one, a farce entitled *THE MODEL OF A WIFE*, he appeared as "Tom."[4]

This is the difference between mothers and sons.

This isn't to say that son love isn't love. Just that mother love—"I shall live for my child"—is a strange bargain one makes quickly and cannot unmake. At least, I would not. Daisy Hay argues that, following Percy Shelley's death, Percy Florence Shelley "provided [Mary Shelley] with a reason to stay alive"; her father-in-law's offer to support Percy Florence if Mary would relinquish all claim to him appalled her, Hay writes, insofar as it suggested she might "part with Percy, the only reason for her continued existence."[5] This is, of course, a problematic way to think about artists who are also mothers. And yet.

To this same grandfather, Percy Florence wrote: "Some ladies friends of Mama who know you, say I am very like you, so I am sure I ought to be good."[6]

In Chelsea Market, there's an old water pipe that has been repurposed as a decorative fountain. Small lights alternate its color from neon blue, to green, to gold. You were looking at it so hard, I almost stood there all day.

In a sort of postscript to a letter to Claire written from Cambridge, Percy Florence asks, "what do you think of my writing—Mummer says it is susceptible of improvement—."

There are two words I love here; one is *Mummer*, the other, *susceptible*.

Mummer: one who murmurs, an actor in a Christmas mime, a bad actor.[7]

Cf. Act 3 of Henry VIII: *Persones . . . disgysed or apparelde as Mommers.* Cf. Pope's *Dunciad*: *Peel'd, patch'd, and pieball'd, linsey-woolsey brothers Grave mummers, sleeveless some, and shirtless others.* Cf. Thomas Carlyle (albeit three years after this letter was penned): *I, for one, will not call the man a Hypocrite! Hypocrite, mummer, the life of him a mere theatricality?*

And then there is *susceptible*. Has the writing improved, or must it improve? That sweet, maternal passive-aggression.

On February 4, 1839, Percy Florence wrote to Claire Clairmont from Cambridge:

> Have you ever read a treatise on Memory—. I should like to see one, But one can easily see what the material theory of memory is, it

brings in vibrations and all that sort of thing, but the immaterial does not disagree with it, it merely gives it a metaphysical form, without memory we should have no consciousness of existence, I fancy you want some such draught as that—. At present I have two existences, There is one which is the apparent one, and with that I am just as the people about me are, gay or studious, or dogged, or sullen, and I partake of the character of them all, and if a person were to see me when I thought nobody was looking I should present a moping existence, My other and internal existence (I can't help being villainously egotistical just now) is all made up of memory—or remembrance or what you will, of that kind of thing—You may always find when I am discontented by the number of letters, that issue from me, directly such a fit seizes me, I make the room so dark as just to give me light to read by, and I go writing letter after letter very voluminously—.

In other words, much like Victor Frankenstein, Percy Florence didn't really like college ("he hates Cambridge now, but not so much as I do— that's impossible"). And much like Percy Florence, and, come to think of it, Victor Frankenstein, I also have two existences, my internal existence now external, at this moment watching the last few minutes of a puppet show on Forty-Second Street.

Later in the letter, Percy Florence writes, "if you will be good enough to read over the part in the letter about the memory I shall be satisfied, I must assume a merry mood, and will hope you are not offended at my making of you in a kind of way a vehicle for my—I hope you will write when you have time, I dare not say more, for I am so afraid of your saying that you will have nothing to do with young people, because they are so unreasonable, so I must strive to be reasonable."[8]

A vehicle for *what*, Percy Florence? In your discourse on memory, an encoded moment of forgetting.

I happen to live in the same neighborhood as the last surviving Beat poet, and sometimes I see her around town with her goddaughter, a middle school student in cut-off shorts and pigtails who gobs glitter makeup on the poet at the local pharmacy counter.

To this child's mother, I remark, *for kids, intimacy is intimacy.*

In his letters to Claire Clairmont, Percy Florence refers to Mary Shelley, sometimes as *Mamma*, sometimes as *the madre*. "Mamma says she is going to write to you tomorrow, and consequently she has nothing to say now—."[9] In one letter, before he signs off, Percy Florence writes, "Mamma wants the rest of the paper so goodbye," and when she takes up the pen, Mary Shelley responds, "The last words are merely an excuse for idleness so don't think I robbed you of any portion of a letter—."[10]

In December 1848, three years before Mary Shelley died of brain cancer, Percy Florence wrote to Claire, "The madre has been so unwell these last few days—with the tic in her head—for her illness seems to change very frequently and oddly—that she cannot write to answer your note . . . The madre will write as soon as she writes to anybody, to you."[11]

While Percy Florence Shelley is not remembered for his literary talent, we know he produced some musical compositions and arrangements, and wrote at least two poems. One of these poems is called *Song of Venus to the Ground Shark*:

I walked on a river's bank
   And Cupid trotted by my side
I saw some damsels lean and lank
   A boat did bring them down the tide

And each a golden arrow had
Each in her breast unfortunate
Each looked at Cupid—silly lad
A doctor as, importunate

But now my little archer son
Pulled out some arrows all of lead
Aimed at the damsels one by one
And split each arrow on the head
And down the tide did swim their bark
Each was glad their arrow was split
For each made them think of a certain ground shark
With an all swallow mouth, a dreadful slit

And glad was I to see my boy
Such noble marks so easily break
But he told me still that a dark eyed toy
The ground shark was giving a dreadful shake

I cast you off, oh lover of many
And lover of none, I send you on
To see if you'll e'er be lover of any
Have a gold arrow from my archer son

Good bye I hope your <u>Valentine</u> dear
Will please you, & she's done so long
I hope she'll last another year
To keep you quiet in your wrong[12]

Cf. Marryat (1834): *There are several kinds of sharks, but the most dangerous are the great white shark and the ground shark.* Ground shark, any species of shark that rarely comes to the surface, often *Echinorrhinus spinosus*, Spinozist allegory, *oh lover of many / And lover of none*, moment of anger, mystery, the dreadful slit between the pain we feel bringing our children into the world and the pain they feel in the world, pain we can't entirely protect them from, even if we give them lead arrows, even if everything turns out OK.

ACKNOWLEDGMENTS

I would like to thank Gianna Mosser and the team at Northwestern University Press, who created space for this project, and my colleagues in the Department of English and Literary Arts, who create an environment in which hybrid work can thrive. To write this book in a community where everyone found its strangeness to be an asset was a unique and generative privilege.

Marjorie Levinson taught me the fine art of time travel; her cameo appearances in this book belie the depth of her continuing influence on all the thinking I do about literature, history, and the mind. *Harvester* takes up a few assignments that have stuck with me from my student days—Re Evitt's challenge to respond to literature creatively as well as critically; Jane Hilberry's injunction to honor one's obsessions; and Yopie Prins's invitation to view genres of literature and of critique as porous, historical constructions. Thanks to Anahid Nersessian and Lily Gurton-Wachter, key interlocutors on the topics of both motherhood and Romanticism, for trusting me with their words, and to Anne McCarthy, who encourages me to reopen the classic discussions of our subfield. "Forgetting" first appeared in *Avidly*, and I am grateful to Sarah Blackwood and Sarah Mesle for their early support of the project. Thanks to Elizabeth Denlinger at the Pforzheimer Collection for her invaluable help, and to Cassie Brand, Brian Shetler, and Patrick Mahoney at Drew University, and Elizabeth Dunn at Duke University, for exacting assistance with archival research. I am grateful to Karla Heeps for help with logistics. Many thanks to Anne Mellor for discussing with me her body of work, and the body, and adding her intellect and humanity to this project. Thanks to Tayana Hardin and Erin Hittesdorf, who helped me get the preface just right; to Billy Stratton, for a debate about methodology that inspired "Self"; and to Brian Kiteley and Bin Ramke, for an accidental tutorial on creative nonfiction that helped to shape the project. I'm grateful to Michelle Faubert for sharing her edition of *Mathilda* with me in advance of its publication, and for generously reading and commenting on a late draft of the book. Sarah Allison and Julia Hansen were the book's wonderful first readers; their illuminating and supportive feedback has helped me carry on. Natalie Garyet introduced me to Lisel Mueller's poetry, and Eleni Sikelianos sent me back to Lorine Niedecker. Nan Z. Da understands that friendship is the purest form of praxis; to list her many edits and encouragements would be to miss the larger point. Stephanie Insley Hershinow provided daily insight and good formalisms. Sarah Ehlers held my hand as I took the leap; she always does. Rebecca Ariel Porte advised me long ago that one should write the book one wants to read, and was a satellite mind while I wrote this one. Chet Lisiecki was there the first time I read *Frankenstein*, and has been there ever since. My brother, Jed Feder, reminds me to be bolder and more honest and more creative whenever possible—and it's always possible. My parents, Rob and Andrea Feder, taught me to value creativity, taught me that caring for a child is a profoundly creative act, and created a world for my child while I was writing. Julia Michie Bruckner, the pediatrician friend mentioned in these pages, is a writer friend, too, and offers both kinds of counsel. I am grateful to Sara and Ezra Rich and to Sheera Talpaz for their support and friendship. Sierra Shaffer just gets it. Thanks to Clara Waldman Federbush and Anna Beck, who left me their stories, and to my grandmothers and my family by marriage, who fill my life with bright links to the past.

Harvester of Hearts was forged in conversation with my students at the University of Denver, several of whom are cited in the book. It's Aric Wheeler who quotes RuPaul in "Forgetting." Kaleigh Nitz and Wren Duggan might recognize their class contributions in "Erasure." The student in "Infant Vows" is Mica Moore. I revised this manuscript while teaching a graduate seminar on the sublime, and want to thank Ashley Colley, Jessica Comola, Carolina Ebeid, Julia Fleming, Elisabeth Kinsey, Molly Kugel-Merkner, Mark Mayer, Thirii Myint, Alison Redman, Natalie Rogers, Sasha Strelitz, Dennis Sweeney, Jennifer Topale, and McCormick Templeman for their unique and fortifying insights as I completed the project, with an extra note of gratitude to McCormick, who helped tremendously during the final weeks of manuscript preparation.

This book belongs to Moshe Kornfeld, and to our son, as does my heart.

NOTES

Preface

1. In *Gut Feminism*, Elizabeth A. Wilson writes, "the gut *is* an organ of mind: it ruminates, deliberates, comprehends." Elizabeth A. Wilson, *Gut Feminism* (Durham, N.C.: Duke University Press, 2015), 5. In a session on pedagogy at the 22nd Annual North American Society for the Study of Romanticism Conference (2014), Marjorie Levinson said, *you can't think without the body; the body is a mind mechanism.*

2. While writing this preface, I referred to "The Mary Wollstonecraft Shelley Chronology and Resource Site," created by Shanon Lawson with Charles E. Robinson, Romantic Circles, March 1998, www.rc.umd.edu.

3. Anne Mellor in conversation with the author, November 8, 2016. In formulating this idea, Mellor cited Paul John Eakin's work in autobiography studies, which includes the books *Living Autobiographically: How We Create Identity in Narrative* (Ithaca, N.Y.: Cornell University Press, 2008); *How Our Lives Become Stories: Making Selves* (Ithaca, N.Y.: Cornell University Press, 1999); and *Fictions in Autobiography: Studies in the Art of Self-Invention* (Princeton, N.J.: Princeton University Press, 1985). Rebecca Solnit writes: "a life isn't a story; it's a whole Milky Way of events and we are forever picking out constellations from it to fit who and where we are." Rebecca Solnit, *The Faraway Nearby* (New York: Penguin, 2014), 246.

4. Solnit, *Faraway Nearby*, 54, 63, 50.

5. Lisel Mueller, "Alive Together," *Alive Together: New and Selected Poems* (Baton Rouge: Louisiana State University Press, 1996), 84. In "The Triumph of Life: Mary Shelley," Mueller writes of Mary Shelley and her children, "For months I wanted to be / with those three small bodies, / to be still in a dark place" and "If I could have chosen my children / and seen them survive / I might have believed in equality, / written your manifestos." Elsewhere in that poem, in a voice she tells us is the voice of Mary Shelley, Mueller writes, "The word survives the body." She writes, "By accident I slid / out of my century / into yours of white-coated men . . ." Lisel Mueller, "The Triumph of Life: Mary Shelley," *Alive Together*, 139–44.

6. Rebecca Traister, "Warning: Abortion's Deadly DIY Past Could Soon Become Its Future," *The Cut*, January 10, 2017, www.thecut.com.

7. Molly Redden, "Texas Has Highest Maternal Mortality Rate in Developed World, Study Finds," *The Guardian*, August 20, 2016.

8. Michelle Faubert, introduction to *Mathilda*, by Mary Shelley (Peterborough, Ontario: Broadview Press, 2017), 9. Faubert's edition of *Mathilda* was in production while I wrote this book, and is now published.

9. Jenny Penberthy, introduction to *Collected Works*, by Lorine Niedecker (Berkeley: University of California Press, 2002), 1, 3, 4, 7.

10. Alexis Pauline Gumbs, *Spill: Scenes of Black Feminist Fugitivity* (Durham, N.C.: Duke University Press, 2016), xi.

11. Gumbs, *Spill*, 129.

12. Jessica Marie Johnson, "'We Need Your Freedom': An Interview with Alexis Pauline Gumbs," *Black Perspectives*, December 13, 2016.

13. Alexis Pauline Gumbs, introduction to part 1, *Revolutionary Mothering: Love on the Front Lines*, ed. Alexis Pauline Gumbs, China Martens, and Mai'a Williams (Oakland, Calif.: PM Press, 2016), 3.

14. Betty T. Bennett argues, "In [Shelley's] relationship with her father-in-law we see another indicator of a woman who broke the social codes even as she smarted under their existence." Bennett explains that Shelley "vigorously negotiated with him through his legal representatives to provide the funds necessary to raise her child . . . Though the allowance was actually a loan, repayable on her inheritance at Sir Timothy's death, to obtain each increase to meet the child's expenses demanded exceptional persistence." Mary Shelley's financial entanglements with her father-in-law put a number of restrictions on her engagement with her late husband's corpus and on her use of the Shelley name. For example, when a review of *The Last Man* named her as the novel's author, Shelley's father-in-law "temporarily withheld the allowance." Betty T. Bennett, *Mary Wollstonecraft Shelley: An Introduction* (Baltimore, Md.: Johns Hopkins University Press, 1998), 65, 77. Hereafter referred to as *MWS: An Introduction*.

15. I am grateful to Jeffrey Robinson for formulating part of this articulation in his blind peer review.

16. Fanny Howe, "Bewilderment," in *The Wedding Dress: Meditations on Word and Life* (Berkeley: University of California Press, 2003), 19.

Chapter 1

Epigraph: This line might refer to the phrase *cor cordium*, heart of hearts, which is inscribed on P. B. Shelley's tomb. Mary Shelley, *The Last Man* (Oxford, Eng.: Oxford World's Classics, 1998), 165, 474. Swinburne's "Cor Cordium" concludes: "Help us for thy free love's sake to be free, / True for thy truth's sake, for thy strength's sake strong, / Till very liberty make clean and fair / The nursing earth as the sepulchral sea." Algernon Charles Swinburne, "Cor Cordium," in *Selections from Swinburne*, ed. H. M. Burton (New York: Cambridge University Press, 1927), 67.

1. Barbara Johnson, "Mary Shelley and Her Circle," in *A Life with Mary Shelley* (Stanford, Calif.: Stanford University Press, 2014), 81.

2. Daisy Hay, *Young Romantics* (New York: Farrar, Straus and Giroux, 2010), 158–59.

3. Jeffrey Jerome Cohen, "Monster Culture: Seven Theses," in *Monster Theory: Reading Culture*, ed. Jeffrey Jerome Cohen (Minneapolis: University of Minnesota Press, 1996), 4.

4. Barbara Johnson, "My Monster/My Self," in *A Life with Mary Shelley*, 24–25.

5. I've pluralized the catchphrase, here. See, among other sources, this interview: "Since I was a kid I've collected catchphrases . . . my favorite would have to be: 'You're born naked and the rest is drag.'" Samuel Fishwick, "RuPaul Charles

Interview: 'You're Born Naked and the Rest Is Drag,'" *Evening Standard*, June 29, 2015.

6. Judith Butler, "Animating Autobiography: Barbara Johnson and Mary Shelley's Monster," in Barbara Johnson, *A Life with Mary Shelley*, 37.

7. Mary Shelley, *Frankenstein*, ed. D. L. Macdonald and Kathleen Scherf (Peterborough, Ontario: Broadview Editions, 2012), 83–84. For substantive variants among the lifetime editions of the novel, see Appendix H. For more on the composition history of *Frankenstein*, see Charles E. Robinson, "*Frankenstein*: Its Composition and Publication," in *The Cambridge Companion to* Frankenstein, ed. Andrew Smith (Cambridge: Cambridge University Press, 2016), 13–25. This book takes the 1818 edition of the novel as its touchstone.

Chapter 2

1. I refer to a page in Dorothy Wordsworth's commonplace book, manuscript item DCMS 120.22 at the Jerwood Center in Grasmere, England. I discuss Dorothy Wordsworth's consolations in more depth in "The Experimental Dorothy Wordsworth," *Studies in Romanticism* 53, no. 4 (2014): 541–59.

2. Betty T. Bennett, "Newly Uncovered Letters and Poems by Mary Wollstonecraft Shelley ('It was my birthday and it pleased me to tell the people so—')," *Keats-Shelley Journal* 46 (1997), 72.

3. Hay, *Young Romantics*, 36, 50.

4. Mary Shelley, *The Letters of Mary Wollstonecraft Shelley*, vol. 1, ed. Betty T. Bennett (Baltimore, Md.: Johns Hopkins University Press, 1980), 10–11.

5. Mary Shelley, *The Journals of Mary Shelley, 1814–1844*, ed. Paula R. Feldman and Diana Scott-Kilvert (Oxford Scholarly Editions Online, 2015), 67.

6. In her unfinished, unpublished biography of Mary Shelley, Betty T. Bennett suggests, "Though they apparently had not named the little girl because of its relatively precarious health, MWS has ~~temporally~~ privately christened her first born: she was 'my' baby." [Chapter 16 of the unpublished biography.] Betty T. Bennett Papers, Byron Society of America Collection, Drew University Library. Here and elsewhere, when I cite Bennett's biography of Mary Shelley, I refer to the typescript versions of the chapters with notes in Bennett's hand. Her archive also includes versions of chapter 19–27 with suggested changes made by her editor.

7. Shelley, *Journals*, 68–69.

8. Ibid., 70, 71.

9. Shelley, *Letters*, 11.

10. Muriel Spark, *Mary Shelley* (Manchester, Eng.: Carcanet, 2013), 38.

11. Ellen Cronan Rose, "Custody Battles: Reproducing Knowledge about 'Frankenstein,'" *New Literary History* 26, no. 4 (1995): 813.

12. Ibid., 819.

13. Ibid., 825–26.

14. Ibid., 826.

15. [Chapter 16 of the unpublished biography.] Betty T. Bennett Papers, Byron Society of America Collection, Drew University Library.

16. I refer to Jacqui Saldana's blog, *Baby Boy Bakery*. This particular statement was from an Instagram post dated April 25, 2015.

17. Yopie Prins and Virginia Jackson, "Lyrical Studies," *Victorian Literature and Culture* 27, no. 2 (1999): 523.

Chapter 3

1. Mary Shelley, *Mathilda* (Brooklyn, N.Y.: Melville House Publishing, 2008), 86. Unless otherwise specified, when I cite *Mathilda*, I refer to the Melville House edition, one of several current reproductions of Elizabeth Nitchie's transcription, which originally appeared as *Mathilda*, ed. Elizabeth Nitchie, Extra Series #3 of *Studies in Philology* (Chapel Hill: The University of North Carolina Press, 1959): 1–80. When I had a question about whether a moment in the text represented an edition-specific typo or was faithful to Nitchie's transcription, I consulted *Mathilda* in Betty T. Bennett and Charles E. Robinson, eds., *The Mary Shelley Reader* (New York: Oxford University Press, 1990), 173–246. I cite the Melville House edition in the main because I wanted to write from the copy of the novella that I have read and reread and taught and re-taught and written all over and earmarked.

2. Ibid., 118.

3. Ibid., 11.

4. Terence Harpold, "'Did You Get Mathilda from Papa?': Seduction Fantasy and the Circulation of Mary Shelley's 'Mathilda,'" *Studies in Romanticism* 28, no. 1 (1989): 64–65.

5. In contrast to other interpretations of Godwin's failure to publish or return the manuscript of *Mathilda*, Bennett suggests that "more probable reasons why neither Godwin nor Mary Shelley on her return to England published *Mathilda*" are, first, to avoid stirring up old rumors about a potentially incestuous relationship involving Mary Shelley, P. B. Shelley, and Claire Clairmont and, second, to adhere to social restrictions regarding appropriate subject matter for women writers rather than create new scandal. Bennett writes, "One almost certain result would be Mary Shelley's loss of Percy Florence Shelley to Sir Timothy Shelley [her father-in-law], who from the outset had wanted total custody." On *Mathilda*'s purpose in Mary Shelley's life, Bennett writes, "The writing of *Mathilda* represented for its author a means of solace derived from the empowering exercise of the imagination. In its secularization of the religious loss-redemption model the prayer ritual is replaced by that of writing. Throughout the novella, Mathilda and Woodville reflexively refer to writing." Bennett, *MWS: An Introduction*, 51–53.

6. Hay, *Young Romantics*, 165.

7. Shelley, *Letters*, 114.

8. Shelley, *Mathilda*, 130.

9. Anne Mellor, *Mary Shelley: Her Life, Her Fiction, Her Monsters* (New York: Routledge, 1988), 199–200.

10. The writer in this paragraph is Lindsey Drager; the project we discussed became the novel *The Lost Daughter Collective* (Ann Arbor: Dzanc Books, 2017).

11. Mary Wollstonecraft, *"Mary, a Fiction" and "The Wrongs of Woman, or Maria,"* ed. Michelle Faubert (Peterborough, Ontario: Broadview Press, 2012), 285.

12. Ibid., 285–87.

13. Mellor, *Mary Shelley*, 1.

14. Jemima goes on to reflect, "Now I look back, I cannot help attributing the greater part of my misery, to the misfortune of having been thrown into the world

without the grand support of life—a mother's affection." Wollstonecraft, *Maria*, 190, 193.

15. Shelley, *Frankenstein*, 65.

16. In this scene, Caroline also tells Victor and Elizabeth that the "expectation" of their marriage "will now be the consolation of your father." Ibid., 72. Notably, in the 1831 edition of *Frankenstein*, Victor and Elizabeth are no longer blood relatives.

17. Wollstonecraft, *Maria*, 202.

18. Ibid.

19. This striking insight about baptism belongs to Claire Boggs.

20. At one point, Maria explains: "By allowing women but one way of rising in the world, the fostering the libertinism of men, society makes monsters of them, and then their ignoble vices are brought forward as a proof of inferiority of intellect." Wollstonecraft, *Maria*, 222–23.

21. Wollstonecraft, *Maria*, 210.

22. Shelley, *Mathilda*, 4.

23. Jack Spicer, "A Red Wheelbarrow," *The Collected Books of Jack Spicer* (Los Angeles: Black Sparrow Press, 1975), 104.

Chapter 4

1. Spark, *Mary Shelley*, 37.

2. Ibid., 52.

3. Ibid., 55–56.

4. Hay, *Young Romantics*, 155.

5. Sandra Boynton, *Hippos Go Berserk!* (New York: Little Simon, 2000).

6. "For one thing, the mother knows the difference between actual destruction and the intention to destroy. She says 'Ow!' when she gets bitten. But she is not disturbed at all by recognizing that the baby wants to eat her. In fact, she feels that this is a compliment, and the way the baby shows excited love. And of course, she is not too easy to eat." D. W. Winnicott, *The Child, the Family, and the Outside World* (Reading, Pa.: Perseus Publishing, 1987), 95.

7. Shelley, *Letters*, 78–79.

8. Ibid., 80.

9. Shelley, *Journals*, 226.

10. Ibid., 226–27.

11. Eve Kosofsky Sedgwick, *Between Men: English Literature and Male Homosocial Desire* (New York: Columbia University Press, 1985), ix.

12. In her edition of *Mathilda*, Faubert connects Godwin's cruel letter chastising Shelley for her depression ("I cannot but consider [your depression] as lowering your character in a memorable degree, & putting you quite among the commonalty & mob of your sex . . ." [it gets worse]) to Mathilda's father's final letter, in which he writes, "believe it, and indeed it is, your duty to be happy." Shelley, *Mathilda*, ed. Faubert, 191, 78.

13. Shelley, *Letters*, 99.

14. Ibid., 100.

15. *Frankenstein*, 118.

16. Shelley, *Letters*, 101, 101, 103.

17. On the matter of P. B. Shelley's heart, Daisy Hay writes, "After Trelawny's ceremony was over, an undignified quarrel broke out between Mary and Hunt

about who should keep Shelley's heart, which somehow miraculously escaped the flames. In fact, the cherished relic was probably Shelley's liver, but Hunt was only persuaded to relinquish it to Mary when Jane Williams persuaded him that Shelley would have been horrified at the idea of his friends quarrelling over one of his organs." Hay, *Young Romantics*, 251.

18. My interest in the contrast between sentiment and maternal passion came out of a conversation with Sarah Knott.

Chapter 5

1. Johann Wolfgang von Goethe, *Elective Affinities*, trans. R. J. Hollingdale (London: Penguin Books, 2005), 52.

2. Ibid., 56.

3. Jon Stone and Michael Smollen, *The Monster at the End of This Book* (New York: Golden Books, 2003).

4. Muriel Spark's copy of *Frankenstein*, The Carl H. Pforzheimer Collection of Shelley and His Circle, The New York Public Library, Astor, Lenox and Tilden Foundations. Spark's copy of *Frankenstein* is the Everyman's Library edition (London: J. M. Dent; New York: E. P. Dutton, 1949), which is based on the 1831 edition of the novel.

5. Richard Herbert Howe, "Max Weber's *Elective Affinities*: Sociology within the Bounds of Pure Reason," *American Journal of Sociology* 84, no. 2 (1978): 367.

6. Ibid.

7. Ibid., 382.

8. N. K. Leacock, "Character, Silence, and the Novel: Walter Benjamin on Goethe's 'Elective Affinities,'" *Narrative* 10, no. 3 (2002): 280.

9. Ibid., 300.

10. Muriel Spark, *Mary Shelley*, xv.

11. Jenny McPhee, "Dopplegängers: Mary Shelley and Muriel Spark," *Bookslut*, December 2011.

12. Spark, *Mary Shelley*, 136. Ellipsis in original.

13. Commenting on a draft of this essay, the novelist McCormick Templeman offered a different take. She explained that, when her children were little, she also wrote scenes where children like them were in danger, because *when writing something that's supposed to be horrifying . . . your subconscious reaches for whatever you find the most horrifying . . . I wonder if it might have been that she put him in there instinctively and then when she realized it, maybe she just named him William. Almost like an offering. Like, here, death, you can take this effigy of William, and I will keep the real little boy.*

14. Rufi Thorpe, "Mother, Writer, Monster, Maid," *Vela Magazine*, June 2016, velamag.com.

15. Rivka Galchen, *Little Labors* (New York: New Directions, 2016), 51.

16. Ibid., 52.

17. Susanna Rustin, "I Lived with Muriel Spark," *The Guardian*, July 5, 2014.

Chapter 6

1. D. W. Winnicott, *The Child*, 24.

2. Ruth Behar, *The Vulnerable Observer* (Boston: Beacon Press, 1996), 165, 174–75.

3. Maureen N. McLane, *Mz N: the serial* (New York: Farrar, Straus and Giroux, 2016), 67.

4. T. S. Eliot, "Tradition and the Individual Talent," in *The Sacred Wood and Major Early Essays* (Mineola, N.Y.: Dover Publications, 1998), 30.

5. Ibid., 33.

6. Ibid., 32.

7. Harriet Monroe, "Shelley," *Poetry* 20, no. 4 (1922): 207.

8. Wilfrid Converse Barton, *Shelley and the New Criticism: The Anatomy of a Critical Misvaluation* (Salzburg: Salzburg Studies in English Literature, 1973), 224.

9. Betty T. Bennett, "The Editor of Letters as Critic: A Denial of 'Blameless Neutrality,'" *Text* 6 (1994): 214.

10. Micah McCrary, "Riding the Blinds: Micah McCrary Interviews Maggie Nelson," *Los Angeles Review of Books*, April 2015.

11. Maggie Nelson, *The Argonauts* (Minneapolis: Graywolf Press, 2015), 19, 21, 33, 140. In her use of the term "ordinary," Nelson riffs on Winnicott's notion of the "Ordinary Devoted Mother." See, for example, D. W. Winnicott, "The Ordinary Devoted Mother," in *Babies and Their Mothers* (Reading, Pa.: Addison-Wesley Publishing Company, Inc., 1987), 3–14.

12. Nelson, *The Argonauts*, 134–35.

13. On becoming an animal giving birth, Claire Jarvis writes, "giving birth was like becoming an animal giving birth." Claire Jarvis, "No One Thinks of Rilke in the Recovery Room," *n + 1*, July 6, 2017. Regarding *Frankenstein*, Paul Youngquist writes, "For Shelley, body is fate," and "Born free we are born fated, fettered to a dying animal." Paul Youngquist, "*Frankenstein*: The Mother, the Daughter, and the Monster," *Philological Quarterly* 70, no. 3 (1991): 344, 355.

14. Winnicott, *The Child*, 165.

15. "Tracy Tynan's 'Wear and Tear,' Plus D. W. Winnicott," *LARB Radio Hour* (podcast), October 6, 2016.

16. Leach continues: "And when, and only when, peace is restored you will have a chance of finding a more permanent solution." Penelope Leach, *Your Baby and Child* (New York: Alfred A. Knopf, 2010), 12.

17. Mary Wollstonecraft, *Letters Written in Sweden, Norway, and Denmark* (New York: Oxford University Press, 2009), 11–12.

18. For more on this topic, see Denise Gigante, *Life: Organic Form and Romanticism* (New Haven, Conn.: Yale University Press, 2009). In her introduction, Gigante writes, "As the concept of vital power sparked a preoccupation with self-generating and self-maintaining form, it quickened the category of the aesthetic, elevating natural researchers into natural philosophers attempting to account for a mysterious power buried deep within the structures of nature. Life scientists focused on the dynamics of organic form in an effort to explain how form emerged and maintained itself, despite the physical laws of an environment that worked, meanwhile, to reduce it to its constituent parts. Aesthetic theorists and practitioners alike focused on the vitality of form, which from the 1790s on had been imbued (by way of Kant's critique of aesthetic and teleological judgment) with the Aristotelian notion of purpose. Yet the problem with the merger of science and aesthetics at the turn of the nineteenth century boiled down to the following: while the sublime object always threatened to exceed formal constraints, when it slid from theory into praxis, from imagined into actual, animated

power, it could also slide out of the sublime and into a distinctly Romantic version of monstrosity," 5.

19. Winnicott, *The Child*, 27.

20. Mary Wollstonecraft, *The Collected Letters of Mary Wollstonecraft*, ed. Janet Todd (New York: Columbia University Press, 2003), 309.

21. Ibid., 429.

22. Barbara Johnson, *Persons and Things* (Cambridge, Mass.: Harvard University Press, 2008), 97.

23. Winnicott, *The Child*, 17.

Chapter 7

1. William Veeder, *Mary Shelley and "Frankenstein": The Fate of Androgyny* (Chicago: University of Chicago Press, 1986), 272.

2. Ibid., 115.

3. Nelson, *The Argonauts*, 90, 87, 13.

4. Veeder, *Mary Shelley*, 116.

5. Pamela Erens, *Eleven Hours* (Portland, Ore.: Tin House Books, 2016), 165.

6. Michael Twinn and Pam Adams, *Pocket Pal PUPPY* (Bridgemead, Swindon UK: Child's Play [International] Ltd, 1995).

7. Merril Bainbridge, "Mouth," *The Garden* (1995).

8. Nelson, *The Argonauts*, 44.

9. Veeder, *Mary Shelley*, 7.

10. "I gasped for breath; and, throwing myself on the body, I exclaimed, 'Have my murderous machinations deprived you also, my dearest Henry, of life? Two I have already destroyed; other victims await their destiny: but you, Clerval, my friend, my benefactor' . . . I was carried out of the room in strong convulsions . . . A fever succeeded to this. I lay for two months on the point of death." Shelley, *Frankenstein*, 183.

11. While Veeder doesn't suggest that Victor Frankenstein is simply in love with Henry, he does collapse literary inquiry and literary history to argue: "Homosexuality is . . . a component of Victor's pursuit of the monster and of Shelley's intense relationships with various men. Percy, Victor, and Robert would all be healthier, however, if homosexual union were their real goal. It would at least establish their ability to relate deeply to someone. But for Robert, Victor, and Percy, the primary significance of the male bond is narcissistic. A man can reflect each of them better than a woman can. Male love is thus one stage closer to the self-embrace which is the true goal ofPrometheans and the chief reason, as we will see soon, for Frankenstein's creation of the monster." Later in the book, Veeder writes, "But communion is limited for Promethean males who slenderly know themselves. Mary knew it in her heart." Veeder, *Mary Shelley*, 88, 209.

12. Ibid., 152.

13. Shelley, *Frankenstein*, 87.

14. James Holt McGavran writes: "Late twentieth-century readers of *Frankenstein* often are half embarrassed, half cynically amused by the erotic undercurrents in Victor's friendships with both Captain Walton and Henry Clerval, yet—apparently because the queer sublime is so totally repressed by the characters—these intimacies constitute safely unsexual male homosocial bondings. No trace of Sedgwick's homosexual panic or Dollimore's perverse dynamic

darkens or distorts their beauty and harmony; all of that seems reserved for the scenes between Victor and his creature." James Holt McGavran, "'Insurmountable Barriers to Our Union': Homosocial Male Bonding, Homosexual Panic, and Death on the Ice in *Frankenstein*," *European Romantic Review* 11, no. 1 (2000): 56. While an intervention in queer-theoretical readings of *Frankenstein* is beyond the scope of this project, I'll just mention that I don't find Victor's love of Henry to be embarrassing, amusing, or particularly safe.

15. Henry Bodkin, "Frankenstein's Monster Would Have Wiped Out Mankind within 4,000 Years, Study Finds," *The Telegraph*, October 2016.

16. Nathaniel J. Dominy and Justin D. Yeakel, "*Frankenstein* and the Horrors of Competitive Exclusion," *BioScience* 67, no. 2 (February 2017): 110.

17. Veeder, *Mary Shelley*, 211.

Chapter 8

1. Shelley, *Journals*, 144.

2. I refer to a Twitter post by @Wordsworthians, the account affiliated with the Wordsworth Trust Romanticism blog (wordsworth.org.uk/blog/), dated November 5, 2016, and to an exchange in the replies between Charlotte Gordon and myself.

3. Miranda Seymour, *Mary Shelley* (London: John Murray, 2000), 174.

4. Jane Blumberg, *Mary Shelley's Early Novels* (Iowa City: University of Iowa Press, 1993), 12.

5. Mary Shelley, "A History of the Jews," in Blumberg, *Early Novels*, 190.

6. Ibid., 191.

7. Blumberg, *Early Novels*, 11–12.

8. Ibid., 29.

9. [Research on Individuals, Box 24, Jewish Issue I and II, 2001.] Betty T. Bennett Papers, Byron Society of America Collection, Drew University Library.

10. Blumberg, *Early Novels*, 19, 29.

11. Shelley, "History," in Blumberg, *Early Novels*, 192.

12. Robert Alter, "Epitaph for a Jewish Magazine: Notes on the 'Menorah Journal,'" *Commentary*, May 1965, 52.

13. Marjorie Levinson, *Wordsworth's Great Period Poems* (Cambridge: Cambridge University Press, 1986), 72–73.

14. David Kaufmann, "Harold's Complaint, or Assimilation in Full Bloom," in *British Romanticism and the Jews: History, Culture, Literature*, ed. Sheila Spector (New York: Palgrave, 2002), 260.

15. Jennifer Plecas, *BAH! Said the Baby* (New York: Philomel Books, 2015).

Chapter 9

1. *Mean Girls*, written by Tina Fey and directed by Mark Waters (2004).

2. Anne K. Mellor, "Reflections on Writing Mary Shelley's Life," in *Mary Wollstonecraft and Mary Shelley: Writing Lives*, ed. Helen M. Buss, D. L. Macdonald, and Anne McWhir (Waterloo, Ontario: Wilfrid Laurier University Press, 2001), 236.

3. Mellor, *Mary Shelley*, 54.

4. Apropos of nothing, here is another girl-fight move: "The complexities of *Frankenstein* . . . open it to many possible readings, among them Gothic, political, biographical, religious, psychological, *anti-male feminist, anti-Godwin*

and anti-Shelley . . . these multiple interpretations have often contradicted one another, dealt only with certain facets of the book, or attributed to Mary Shelley concepts that have more to do with the bias of the particular critic than with the author herself" (emphasis mine). Bennett finds in these divergent interpretations a through-line dealing with power and responsibility, a thematic Bennett also locates at the crux of *Mathilda*. Bennett, *MWS: An Introduction*, 30, 48.

5. See Elseline Hoekzema et al., "Pregnancy Leads to Long-Lasting Changes in Human Brain Structure," *Nature Neuroscience* 20 (2017), 287–96. Published online December 19, 2016.

Chapter 10

1. Shelley, *Mathilda*, 3, 4.

2. Hargrave Hands, *Duckling Sees* (New York: Grosset & Dunlap, 1985). Ellipsis in original.

3. Shelley, *Mathilda*, 4.

4. Ibid., 5.

5. Ibid., 8.

6. Ibid., 9.

7. Ibid.

8. Ibid., 11.

9. Ibid.

10. Elizabeth Nitchie, *Mary Shelley, Author of "Frankenstein"* (New Brunswick, N.J.: Rutgers University Press, 1953), 11.

11. Charlotte Gordon, *Romantic Outlaws: The Extraordinary Lives of Mary Wollstonecraft and Mary Shelley* (New York: Random House, 2015), 327.

12. Nitchie, *Mary Shelley*, 11.

13. Ibid., 11–12. Second ellipsis in original.

14. Shelley, *Mathilda*, 16–17.

15. Jane Bennett, *Vibrant Matter: A Political Ecology of Things* (Durham, N.C.: Duke University Press, 2010), viii, ix, vii.

16. See William Wordsworth, "We Are Seven," *Lyrical Ballads: 1798 and 1800*, ed. Michael Gamer and Dahlia Porter (Peterborough, Ontario: Broadview Editions, 2008), 100–102.

17. Shelley, *Mathilda*, 12, 13, 13.

18. Gordon, *Romantic Outlaws*, 325. To call these "deathbed words spoken" by Wollstonecraft is a bit misleading; Wollstonecraft's probable last written words were "Mrs. Blenkinsop [the midwife] tells me that I am in the most natural state, and can promise me a safe delivery—But that I must have a little patience." Wollstonecraft, *Letters*, 437.

Chapter 11

1. ["'Frankenstein,' A Play by Betty T. Bennett (Adapted from Mary Shelley's Novel, <u>Frankenstein</u>), Revised March 14, 1988.] Betty T. Bennett Papers, Byron Society of America Collection, Drew University Library.

2. Betty T. Bennett, "Feminism and Editing Mary Wollstonecraft Shelley: The Editor And?/Or? The Text," in *Palimpsest: Editorial Theory in the Humanities*, ed. George Bornstein and Ralph G. Williams (Ann Arbor: University of Michigan Press, 1992), 67–96; 91–92.

3. [Chapter 17 of the unpublished biography.] Betty T. Bennett Papers, Byron Society of America Collection, Drew University Library.

4. ["The Lost Journal."] Betty T. Bennett Papers, Byron Society of America Collection, Drew University Library, 24.

5. Ibid., 5.

6. Ibid., 6–7.

7. Ibid., 7.

8. Ibid., 12.

9. Ibid., 23.

10. Ibid.

11. Ibid., 34.

12. Ibid., 32.

Chapter 12

1. Graham Allen, *Mary Shelley* (New York: Palgrave, 2008), 41. *Mathilda* is sometimes spelled "*Matilda*" by critics, and even by Shelley herself; I have maintained this inconsistency in quoted material. For more information, see Michelle Faubert's "Note on the Text" in the Broadview edition of *Mathilda* (Shelley, *Mathilda*, ed. Faubert, 38).

2. E. B. Murray, introduction to *Percy Bysshe Shelley Volume IV: A Facsimile of Bodleian MS. Shelley d. 1, part one* (New York: Garland Publishing, 1988), xxxi, xxxiii.

3. Ibid., xxxii.

4. I should note that Faubert interprets *Mathilda* as an intervention in Romantic-era debates about the right to take one's life. See the introduction and Appendix A in the Broadview edition of *Mathilda* as well as Michelle Faubert, "A Family Affair: Ennobling Suicide in Mary Shelley's *Matilda*," *Essays in Romanticism* 20 (2013): 101–28. In an essay she wrote for a spring 2017 Romantic literature course, Jacquelyn Sublett suggests that the creature's promised suicide in *Frankenstein*—with its "exult[ing] in agony" (*Frankenstein*, 221) and its correspondence to the continuation of human life—might be likened to childbirth.

5. Betty T. Bennett, "Biographical Imaginings and Mary Shelley's (Extant and Missing) Correspondence," in *Mary Wollstonecraft and Mary Shelley: Writing Lives*, ed. Helen M. Buss, D. L. Macdonald, and Anne McWhir (Waterloo, Ontario: Wilfrid Laurier University Press, 2001), 222.

6. Elizabeth Nitchie, "Mary Shelley's *Mathilda*: An Unpublished Story and Its Biographical Significance," *Studies in Philology* 40 (1943): 448.

7. Ibid., 453.

8. Murray, introduction, xxxi–xxxii.

9. Tilottama Rajan, "Mary Shelley's *Mathilda*: Melancholy and the Political Economy of Romanticism," *Studies in the Novel* 26, no. 2 (1994): 46.

10. Mary Shelley, facsimile of the manuscript draft of Mathilda, *Percy Bysshe Shelley Volume IV: A Facsimile of Bodleian MS. Shelley d. 1, part one*, ed. E. B. Murray (New York: Garland Publishing: 1988), 266–67.

11. Nitchie, Mary Shelley's *Mathilda*, 449. Some scholars, Faubert among them, think Shelley continued revising *Mathilda* until February 1820. See the chronologies in the Broadview editions of *Mathilda* and *Frankenstein*, and Lawson and Robinson's *Chronology and Resource Site*.

12. Mary Wollstonecraft, "The Cave of Fancy," in *The Works of Mary Wollstonecraft*, vol. 1, ed. Janet Todd and Marilyn Butler (New York: New York University Press, 1989), 197. On "The Cave of Fancy," Faubert writes, "In Wollstonecraft's little-known narrative, a purgatory-bound soul tells of her hopeless love for a man with whom she wishes to be rejoined after her period of purification. Mathilda reveals a comparable wish throughout her tale . . . Both characters view their present state of existence as a purgatory through which they must pass in order to be united to a man whom they cannot love on earth." Faubert, introduction to *Mathilda*, 22.

13. Mary Shelley, "On Ghosts," *The Mary Shelley Reader*, ed. Betty T. Bennett and Charles E. Robinson (New York: Oxford University Press, 1990), 336.

14. Ibid., 336.

15. Thorpe, *Writer, Mother.*

16. "Unless we are ready to separate—unless we are ready to leave [our mother] and be left—anything is better than separation." Judith Viorst, *Necessary Losses* (New York: Free Press, 2002), 22.

17. Shelley, *Mathilda*, 3.

18. Ibid., 132.

19. Ibid., 133.

Chapter 13

1. Shelley, *Mathilda*, 25.

2. Ibid., 28.

3. Ibid., 23.

4. Ibid., 26.

5. Ibid., 25.

6. Ibid., 29–30.

7. Ibid., 30.

8. Olivia Thomas, Claire Boggs, Evan Morsch, Madison Bolotin, and Grace Hansen developed this argument during a spring 2017 meeting of "Literary Inquiry: Monster Narratives."

9. Shelley, *Mathilda*, 29.

10. D. W. Winnicott, *Babies and Their Mothers* (Reading, Pa.: Addison-Wesley Publishing Company, Inc., 1987), 36–37.

11. Ibid., 37.

12. Shelley, *Mathilda*, 15.

13. *Dirty Dancing*, written by Eleanor Bergstein and directed by Emile Ardolino (1987).

14. Making an inverted but related point, Mellor writes: "Perhaps someday an editor will give us the manuscript [of *Frankenstein*] Mary Shelley actually wrote, cleansed of [her husband's] elaborations." Mellor, *Mary Shelley*, 62.

15. John Lauritsen, series of emails to the NASSR listserv, November 16, 2016. In these emails, Lauritsen refers to his argument in *The Man Who Wrote Frankenstein* (New York: Pagan Press, 2007).

16. Shelley, *Mathilda*, 25 (emphasis mine).

Chapter 14

Epigraph: Barbara Johnson, *Mary Shelley and Her Circle*, 103–4.

1. Barbara Johnson, *The Feminist Difference* (Cambridge, Mass.: Harvard University Press, 1998), 157, 159, 160.
2. Ibid., 163.
3. Ibid., 164.
4. Johnson, "My Monster/My Self," 26.
5. Shoshana Felman, "Barbara Johnson's Last Book," in *A Life with Mary Shelley*, 156.
6. Ibid., 148.
7. Ibid., 138.
8. Johnson, *Mary Shelley and Her Circle*, 80.
9. Johnson, *My Monster/My Self*, 24.
10. Felman, "Last Book," 145.
11. Ibid., 128.
12. Johnson, *Mary Shelley and Her Circle*, 90–91.
13. Barbara Johnson, *Mother Tongues* (Cambridge, Mass.: Harvard University Press, 2003), 77.
14. Ibid., 78, 79.
15. This is possibly my favorite moment in any novel. Frankenstein has hiked to the summit of Montanvert, the deaths of William and Justine heavy on his mind: "My heart, which was before sorrowful, now swelled with something like joy; I exclaimed—'Wandering spirits, if indeed ye wander, and do not rest in your narrow beds, allow me this faint happiness, or take me, as your companion, away from the joys of life.'" And then he sees him, the creature, large and swift, approaching. Frankenstein's "trembl[ing]" and screaming, threatening: "Begone, vile insect! or rather stay, that I may trample you to dust! and, oh, that I could, with the extinction of your miserable existence, restore those victims whom you have so diabolically murdered!" There's a little irony in that phrase, *miserable existence*—Frankenstein can't realize just how miserable that existence has been, never quite accepts the blame for that misery. But the creature's opening line—"I expected this reception"—tells us he is educated in the complex functionality of monster narratives. By this point, he's realized what kind of book he's in. Shelley, *Frankenstein*, 117–18.
16. Rachel Cusk, *A Life's Work* (New York: Picador, 2001), 205.
17. Ibid., 206.
18. Johnson, *Mary Shelley and Her Circle*, 58.
19. Ibid., 60.

Chapter 15
1. Shelley, *Mathilda*, 29, 30.
2. Ibid., 37.
3. Ibid., 36–37.
4. Winnicott, *The Child*, 116.
5. Ibid., 117.
6. Shelley, *Mathilda*, 35.
7. Wollstonecraft, *Letters*, 436.
8. Shelley, *Mathilda*, 36.
9. Shelley, *Mathilda*, ed. Faubert, 59.
10. Ibid., 35. Shelley quotes Francis Beaumont and John Fletcher's 1647 *The Captain*, a comedy with some thematic treatment of incest.

11. Ibid., 36–44 passim.

12. Ibid., 46–49 passim.

13. Ibid., 49–52 passim.

14. This scene of coming together trespasses, criminally, on Mathilda's childhood fantasy of running away, disguising herself as a boy, and looking for her father: "My imagination hung upon the scene of recognition; his miniature, which I should continually wear exposed on my breast, would be the means." Shelley, *Mathilda*, 20. When she hears of William Frankenstein's death, and thinks of how the child had persuaded her to let him wear "a very valuable miniature" of his mother, Elizabeth decides the treasure must have "urged the murderer to the deed" and cries, "'O God! I have murdered my darling infant!'" (This same miniature, planted on Justine, performs the creature's second murder for him.) Shelley, *Frankenstein*, 96.

15. Regina Spektor, "Bleeding Heart," *Remember Us to Life* (2016).

16. Shelley, *Mathilda*, 51.

17. See the chapter "Fathers and Daughters, or 'A Sexual Education'" in Mellor, *Mary Shelley*, 177–212, as well as Mellor's discussions of maternal anxiety, e.g., "Am I capable of raising a healthy, normal child? . . . Could I kill it? Could it kill *me*" (41) and "*even if I love and nurture my child . . . I may still produce a monster—and who is responsible for that?*" (50).

18. Spark, *Mary Shelley*, 123–24. Ellipses in original.

19. Sarah Manguso, *Ongoingness: The End of a Diary* (Minneapolis: Graywolf Press, 2015), 11.

20. Shelley, *Mathilda*, 55–69 passim.

21. Ibid., 8, 11.

Chapter 16

1. Ellen Moers, "Female Gothic," *Literary Women: The Great Writers* (New York: Oxford University Press, 1985), 91, 92.

2. Ibid., 92.

3. Ibid., 94–99 passim.

4. "That's furniture which the spooks can move around any way they want to . . . But the only way to find out what furniture you need is to lack it. You go to a place, and the green Martian spook doesn't find anything in the room he can possibly sit in. This tells the poet, for chrissakes get another chair for the room. And I certainly think that a poet ought to supply as much furniture as possible but then ought to be very careful about not saying, 'oh *please*, sit down in this new armchair I've just gotten.'" Jack Spicer, *The House That Jack Built: The Collected Lectures of Jack Spicer*, ed. Peter Gizzi (Middletown, Conn.: Wesleyan University Press, 1998), 81–82.

5. Shelley, *Frankenstein*, 51.

6. Ibid., 64.

7. Ibid., 83.

8. Ibid.

9. Ibid., 84.

10. Galchen, *Little Labors*, 39–40.

11. Ibid., 38.

12. Adam Zagajewski, "Epithalamium," *Eternal Enemies* (New York: Farrar, Straus and Giroux, 2008), 88.

13. Shelley, *Frankenstein*, 84.

14. Ibid.

15. Shelley, *Frankenstein*, 217. Regarding this pun, Barbara Claire Freeman writes: "The analogy between forbidden bodies and books is heightened by the fact that, although his mother's death postpones Victor's departure for the University of Ingolstadt, what he finds there becomes a substitute for her, an alma mater. Shortly after he arrives Victor sets out to find a way of making mothers irrelevant . . . Just as the knowledge Victor pursues in the hope of gaining access to the secrets of life brings him into intimate proximity to death, so the sublimation of Victor's desire for the mother produces a monstrous 'mummy' who is responsible for the death of mothers. In this case the fruits of reason serve not merely to scapegoat the feminine but to destroy it." Barbara Claire Freeman, *The Feminine Sublime: Gender and Excess in Women's Fiction* (Berkeley: University of California Press, 1997), 83.

16. Kevin Cadogan and Stephan Jenkins, "How's It Going to Be," *Third Eye Blind* (1997).

17. Maurice Sendak, *Where the Wild Things Are* (New York: Harper Collins, 2012). Sendak's "wild thing" comes from a Yiddish phrase, *vilde chaya*. See John Cech, *Angels and Wild Things: The Archetypal Poetics of Maurice Sendak* (University Park: Pennsylvania State University Press, 1995).

18. Margaret Wise Brown, *Big Red Barn* (New York: HarperFestival, 1995).

19. Anne E. Fernald, "In the Great Green Room: Margaret Wise Brown and Modernism," *Public Books*, November 2015, www.publicbooks.org.

20. Sendak, *Where the Wild Things Are*.

21. Shelley, *Frankenstein*, 120–21.

Chapter 17

1. Lin-Manuel Miranda, "Dear Theodosia," *Hamilton* (2015).

2. Nancy Isenberg, "Liberals Love Alexander Hamilton. But Aaron Burr Was a Real Progressive Hero," *Washington Post*, March 30, 2016.

3. On Burr's return to Theodosia, Bennett writes, "Burr wanted to go home earlier that winter but the American consul held up his return; at least once he tried to leave under an assumed name. His other obstacle was money. Desperate, he asked the Godwins to help him sell his ring-watch, which failed because 'distressed émigrés from France and Germany' had flooded that market. Finally, with both cash and permission in hand, before taking his fond farewell, he tried to settle his debts to the Godwins. He owed them some £5 or £6, but putting his need before their own, they refused the money." Bennett cites Aaron Burr, *The private journal of Aaron Burr during his residence of four years in Europe: with selections from his correspondence*, vol. 2 (New York: Harper, 1838), 357. Among her handwritten notes on the chapter draft is the statement: "Need bigger bang at end of this chapter." [Chapter 5 of the unpublished biography.] Betty T. Bennett Papers, Byron Society of America Collection, Drew University Library.

4. Aaron Burr, *The private journal of Aaron Burr*, 249, 337, 365.

5. Martin Garrett, *A Mary Shelley Chronology* (New York: Palgrave, 2002), 8.

6. Ibid.
7. Isenberg, "Liberals."
8. Shelley, *Frankenstein*, 219.
9. Ibid., 218.
10. Cohen, "Monster Culture," 20.
11. Jeffrey Jerome Cohen, "The Story I Want to Tell," *In the Middle* (blog), November 2016.
12. I was actually thinking of Michael Twinn and Pam Adams, *LION: A Child's Play Pocket Pal* (Bridgemead, Swindon UK: Child's Play [International] Ltd, 2000).
13. Lin-Manuel Miranda, "Aaron Burr, Sir," *Hamilton* (2015).

Chapter 18

1. Shelley, *Frankenstein*, 220.
2. Barbara Johnson, "Apostrophe, Animation, and Abortion," in *The Barbara Johnson Reader*, ed. Judith Butler (Durham, N.C.: Duke University Press, 2014), 225.
3. Ibid., 224.
4. Ibid., 227.
5. Ibid., 231–32.
6. Shelley, *Frankenstein*, 164.
7. Ibid., 165.
8. Ibid., 168.
9. Nancy J. Vickers, "Diana Described: Scattered Woman and Scattered Rhyme," *Critical Inquiry* 8, no. 2 (Winter 1981): 266.
10. Ibid., 269, 273.
11. Ibid., 276–77.
12. Shelley, *Frankenstein*, 172–73.
13. Ibid., 173.
14. Ibid.
15. Ibid., 174.
16. Ibid., 174–75.
17. Tobin Siebers, "Broken Beauty: Disability and Art Vandalism," *Michigan Quarterly Review* 41, no. 2 (2002): 223–24.
18. Shelley, *Frankenstein*, 176.
19. Ibid., 175–76.
20. Ibid., 218.
21. Roland Barthes, "The Death of the Author," in *Image Music Text*, trans. Stephen Heath (New York: Hill and Wang, 1978), 148.
22. Shelley, *Frankenstein*, 178.
23. Ibid., 178–79.

Chapter 19

1. [Research on Individuals, Box 22 (Elena Shelley).] Betty T. Bennett Papers, Byron Society of America Collection, Drew University Library. This research file includes photocopies from Newman Ivey White's archives (Newman Ivey White Papers, Duke University Archives, David M. Rubenstein Rare Book & Manuscript Library, Duke University). Regarding his research on Elena Adelaide

Shelley, White writes: "In October 1936, through the courtesy of Mr. Coert Du Bois, American Consul-General at Naples, I engaged Professor Alberto Tortaglione to search the birth-records and death-records of Naples for the mysterious 'Neapolitan ward' mentioned in Shelley's letters of June 1820 to Mr. and Mrs. Gisborne. The following documents were found [and follow in an appendix], for which Professor Tortaglione supplied the English translation." Newman Ivey White, *Shelley*, vol. 2 (New York: Alfred A. Knopf, 1940), 546.

2. [Research on Individuals, Box 22 (Elena Shelley).] Betty T. Bennett Papers, Byron Society of America Collection, Drew University Library.

3. Gordon, *Romantic Outlaws*, 245.

4. Matthew Borushko, review of *Percy Bysshe Shelley: A Biography*, by James Bieri, in *Studies in Romanticism* 51, no. 1 (2012): 117.

5. In addition to Borushko's review, see James Bieri, *Percy Bysshe Shelley: A Biography* (Baltimore, Md.: Johns Hopkins University Press, 2008).

6. Miranda Seymour, *Mary Shelley*, 227.

7. Gordon, *Romantic Outlaws*, 298.

8. Shelley, *Frankenstein*, 154.

9. Ibid.

10. Ibid.

11. Gordon, *Romantic Outlaws*, 243.

12. Ibid., 240–41.

13. [Chapter 22, the unpublished biography.] Betty T. Bennett Papers, Byron Society of America Collection, Drew University Library.

14. Shelley, *Frankenstein*, 154.

15. Ibid., 90.

Chapter 20

1. Shelley, *Journals*, 134.

2. Ibid., 293.

3. Shelley, *Letters*, 53.

4. Ibid., 91, 93.

5. John Keats, *The Complete Poems* (New York: Penguin Classics, 1977), 99.

6. Gordon, *Romantic Outlaws*, 275.

7. Barbara Johnson, *Mother Tongues*, 66.

8. Rainer Maria Rilke, *Selected Poems*, trans. C. F. MacIntyre (Berkeley: University of California Press, 1940), 93.

9. Percy Bysshe Shelley. "My Lost William (To William Shelley)," in *The Shelley-Godwin Archive*, MS HM 2177, 46r (rev.). Retrieved from http://shelleygodwinarchive.org/sc/hu/to_william/#/p1.

10. Shelley, *Letters*, 93.

11. Gordon, *Romantic Outlaws*, 302.

12. Ibid., 303.

Chapter 22

1. [Correspondence regarding Clara Everina Shelley's burial site, 1998–1999.] Betty T. Bennett Papers, Byron Society of America Collection, Drew University Library.

2. Bennett, *MWS: An Introduction*, 46.

3. Shelley, *Frankenstein*, 95–96.

4. Ibid., 97.

5. Ibid., 111.

6. [Chapter 25, the unpublished biography.] Betty T. Bennett Papers, Byron Society of America Collection, Drew University Library.

7. Spicer, *The Collected Books*, 177.

8. Shelley, *Frankenstein*, 220–21.

Chapter 23

1. Shelley, *Mathilda*, 8, 91.

2. In a letter to Maria Gisborne dated August 15, 1822, Mary Shelley writes of the process by which she learned of her husband's death: "I trembled all over— Jane [Williams, whose partner drowned with P. B. Shelley] read it—'Then it is all over!' she said. 'No, my dear Jane,' I cried, 'it is not all over, but this suspense is dreadful—come with me, we will go to Leghorn, we will post to be swift & learn our fate.' We crossed to Lerici, despair in our hearts; they raised our spirits there by telling us that no accident had been heard of & that it must have been known &c—but still our fear was great—& without resting we posted to Pisa It must have been fearful to see us—two poor, wild, aghast creatures—driving (like Matilda) towards the <u>sea</u> to learn if we were to be for ever doomed to misery." Shelley, *Letters*, 247.

3. Shelley, *Mathilda*, 73–78 passim.

4. Ibid., 81–87 passim.

5. Ibid., 90–100 passim.

6. Ibid., 108.

7. Ibid., 103, 119, 120, 105.

8. Ibid., 114.

9. Ibid., 130–32.

10. Ibid., 133.

11. Ibid.

12. Ibid., 72. To undergraduate students surprised to find that *Frankenstein* lacked the dramatic scene of animation they'd seen in various filmic adaptations of the novel, Mark Mayer pointed out that this incantation, combined with the image of lightning striking a tree, offered some of the key motifs they had expected.

Chapter 24

1. In this section, I think with Charlotte Gordon's interpretation of events: "Mary urged Shelley to tell Byron to adopt Alba. She knew that without the child, Claire would need less support and would be better able to strike out on her own. Claire did not want to part with Alba, but she nursed a secret hope that when Byron met his new daughter and saw how beautiful she was, he would fall back in love with her. Shelley obliged his wife by painting a pretty domestic scene in a letter to Byron to try to persuade him to assume responsibility for Alba." Gordon, *Romantic Outlaws*, 248.

Chapter 25

Epigraph: [Introductions to the unpublished biography.] Betty T. Bennett Papers, Byron Society of America Collection, Drew University Library.

1. Hay, *Young Romantics*, 240.

2. Nora Ephron, "Nora Ephron '62 Addressed the Graduates in 1996," Wellesley College website (commencement archives).

3. Wollstonecraft, *Maria*, 215.

Chapter 26

1. In the Whitall-Clawson album of Shelleyana. The archival material cited in this chapter belongs to The Carl H. Pforzheimer Collection of Shelley and His Circle, The New York Public Library, Astor, Lenox and Tilden Foundations.

2. Autograph letter to William Stedman, February 7, 1851. Shelleyana 1020.

3. Autograph letter to Leigh Hunt, February 6, 1851. Shelleyana 0074.

4. Album *orné* of Percy Florence Shelley, leaf 7 (verso), mounted broadside playbill for Boscombe Theatre.

5. Hay, *Young Romantics*, 258, 269.

6. Autograph letter to Sir Timothy Shelley, November 12, 1830. Shelleyana 0550.

7. The denotations and etymological quotes cited in this essay are from the Oxford English Dictionary, 3rd ed. (June 2009).

8. Autograph letter to Claire Clairmont, February 4, 1839. Shelleyana 1051.

9. Autograph letter to Claire Clairmont, October 27, 1842. Shelleyana 1053.

10. Autograph letter to Claire Clairmont, January 23 [no year]. Shelleyana 1054/MWS 0413.

11. Autograph letter to Claire Clairmont, December 4, 1848. Shelleyana 1056.

12. Holograph poems (no date). Shelleyana 1060.

BIBLIOGRAPHY

Allen, Graham. *Mary Shelley*. New York: Palgrave, 2008.

Alter, Robert. "Epitaph for a Jewish Magazine: Notes on the *Menorah Journal*." *Commentary*, May 1965.

Barthes, Roland. *Image Music Text*. Translated by Stephen Heath. New York: Hill and Wang, 1978.

Barton, Wilfrid Converse. *Shelley and the New Criticism: The Anatomy of a Critical Misvaluation*. Salzburg: Salzburg Studies in English Literature, 1973.

Behar, Ruth. *The Vulnerable Observer*. Boston: Beacon Press, 1996.

Bennett, Betty T. "Biographical Imaginings and Mary Shelley's (Extant and Missing) Correspondence." In *Mary Wollstonecraft and Mary Shelley: Writing Lives*, edited by Helen M. Buss, D. L. Macdonald, and Anne McWhir, 217–31. Waterloo, Ontario: Wilfrid Laurier University Press, 2001.

———. "The Editor of Letters as Critic: A Denial of 'Blameless Neutrality.'" *Text* 6 (1994): 213–23.

———. "Feminism and Editing Mary Wollstonecraft Shelley: The Editor And?/ Or? The Text." In *Palimpsest: Editorial Theory in the Humanities*, edited by George Bornstein and Ralph G. Williams, 67–96. Ann Arbor: University of Michigan Press, 1992.

———. *Mary Wollstonecraft Shelley: An Introduction*. Baltimore, Md.: Johns Hopkins University Press, 1998.

———. "Newly Uncovered Letters and Poems by Mary Wollstonecraft Shelley ('It was my birthday and it pleased me to tell the people so—')." *Keats-Shelley Journal* 46 (1997): 51–74.

Bennett, Jane. *Vibrant Matter: A Political Ecology of Things*. Durham, N.C.: Duke University Press, 2010.

Blumberg, Jane. *Mary Shelley's Early Novels*. Iowa City: University of Iowa Press, 1993.

Bodkin, Henry. "Frankenstein's Monster Would Have Wiped Out Mankind within 4,000 Years, Study Finds." *The Telegraph*, October 2016.

Borushko, Matthew. Review of *Percy Bysshe Shelley: A Biography*, by James Bieri. *Studies in Romanticism* 51, no. 1 (2012): 114–18.

Boynton, Sandra. *Hippos Go Berserk!* New York: Little Simon, 2000.

Brown, Margaret Wise. *Big Red Barn*. New York: HarperFestival, 1995.

Burr, Aaron. *The private journal of Aaron Burr during his residence of four years in Europe: with selections from his correspondence*, volume 2. New York: Harper, 1838.

Butler, Judith. "Animating Autobiography: Barbara Johnson and Mary Shelley's Monster," in Barbara Johnson, *A Life with Mary Shelley*, 37–50. Stanford, Calif.: Stanford University Press, 2014.

Cohen, Jeffrey Jerome. "Monster Culture: Seven Theses." In *Monster Theory: Reading Culture*, edited by Jeffrey Jerome Cohen, 3–25. Minneapolis: University of Minnesota Press, 1996.

Cusk, Rachel. *A Life's Work*. New York: Picador, 2001.

Dominy, Nathaniel J., and Justin D. Yeakel. "*Frankenstein* and the Horrors of Competitive Exclusion." *BioScience* 67, no. 2 (February 2017): 107–10.

Eliot, T. S. *The Sacred Wood and Major Early Essays*. Mineola, N.Y.: Dover Publications, 1998.

Ephron, Nora. "Nora Ephron '62 Addressed the Graduates in 1996." Wellesley College website (commencement archives).

Erens, Pamela. *Eleven Hours*. Portland, Ore.: Tin House Books, 2016.

Faubert, Michelle. Introduction to *Mathilda*, by Mary Shelley, 9–33. Peterborough, Ontario: Broadview Press, 2017.

Felman, Shoshana. "Barbara Johnson's Last Book," in Barbara Johnson, *A Life with Mary Shelley*. Stanford: Stanford University Press, 2014.

Fernald, Anne E. "In the Great Green Room: Margaret Wise Brown and Modernism." *Public Books*, November 2015. www.publicbooks.org.

Fishwick, Samuel. "RuPaul Charles Interview: 'You're Born Naked and the Rest Is Drag.'" *Evening Standard*, June 29, 2015.

Freeman, Barbara Claire. *The Feminine Sublime: Gender and Excess in Women's Fiction*. Berkeley: University of California Press, 1997.

Galchen, Rivka. *Little Labors*. New York: New Directions, 2016.

Garrett, Martin. *A Mary Shelley Chronology*. New York: Palgrave, 2002.

Gigante, Denise. *Life: Organic Form and Romanticism*. New Haven, Conn.: Yale University Press, 2009.

Goethe, Johann Wolfgang von. *Elective Affinities*. Translated by R. J. Hollingdale. London: Penguin Books, 2005.

Gordon, Charlotte. *Romantic Outlaws: The Extraordinary Lives of Mary Wollstonecraft and Mary Shelley*. New York: Random House, 2015.

Gumbs, Alexis Pauline. Introduction to part 1, *Revolutionary Mothering: Love on the Front Lines*, 3–4. Edited by Alexis Pauline Gumbs, China Martens, and Mai'a Williams. Oakland, Calif.: PM Press, 2016.

———. *Spill: Scenes of Black Feminist Fugitivity*. Durham, N.C.: Duke University Press, 2016.

Hands, Hargrave. *Duckling Sees*. New York: Grosset & Dunlap, 1985.

Harpold, Terence. "'Did You Get Mathilda from Papa?': Seduction Fantasy and the Circulation of Mary Shelley's 'Mathilda.'" *Studies in Romanticism* 28, no. 1 (1989): 49–67.

Hay, Daisy. *Young Romantics*. New York: Farrar, Straus and Giroux, 2010.

Howe, Fanny. *The Wedding Dress: Meditations on Word and Life*. Berkeley: University of California Press, 2003.

Howe, Richard Herbert. "Max Weber's Elective Affinities: Sociology within the Bounds of Pure Reason." *American Journal of Sociology* 84, no. 2 (1978): 366–85.

Isenberg, Nancy. "Liberals Love Alexander Hamilton. But Aaron Burr Was a Real Progressive Hero." *Washington Post*, March 2016.

Jarvis, Claire. "No One Thinks of Rilke in the Recovery Room." *n + 1*, July 6, 2017.

Johnson, Barbara. "Apostrophe, Animation, and Abortion." In *The Barbara Johnson Reader*, edited by Judith Butler, 217–33. Durham, N.C.: Duke University Press, 2014.

———. *The Feminist Difference*. Cambridge, Mass.: Harvard University Press, 1998.

———. *A Life with Mary Shelley*. Stanford, Calif.: Stanford University Press, 2014.

———. *Mother Tongues*. Cambridge, Mass.: Harvard University Press, 2003.

———. *Persons and Things*. Cambridge, Mass.: Harvard University Press, 2008.

Johnson, Jessica Marie. "'We Need Your Freedom': An Interview with Alexis Pauline Gumbs." *Black Perspectives*, December 13, 2016.

Kaufmann, David. "Harold's Complaint, or Assimilation in Full Bloom." In *British Romanticism and the Jews: History, Culture, Literature*, edited by Sheila Spector, 249–63. New York: Palgrave, 2002.

Keats, John. *The Complete Poems*. New York: Penguin Classics, 1977.

Lawson, Shanon, with Charles E. Robinson. "The Mary Wollstonecraft Shelley Chronology and Resource Site." Romantic Circles, March 1998. www.rc.umd .edu.

Leach, Penelope. *Your Baby and Child*. New York: Alfred A. Knopf, 2010.

Leacock, N. K. "Character, Silence, and the Novel: Walter Benjamin on Goethe's 'Elective Affinities.'" *Narrative* 10, no. 3 (2002): 277–306.

Levinson, Marjorie. *Wordsworth's Great Period Poems*. Cambridge: Cambridge University Press, 1986.

Manguso, Sarah. *Ongoingness: The End of a Diary*. Minneapolis: Graywolf Press, 2015.

McCrary, Micah. "Riding the Blinds: Micah McCrary Interviews Maggie Nelson." *Los Angeles Review of Books*, April 2015.

McGavran, James Holt. "'Insurmountable Barriers to Our Union': Homosocial Male Bonding, Homosexual Panic, and Death on the Ice in *Frankenstein*." *European Romantic Review* 11, no. 1 (2000): 46–67.

McLane, Maureen N. *Mz N: the serial*. New York: Farrar, Straus and Giroux, 2016.

McPhee, Jenny. "Dopplegängers: Mary Shelley and Muriel Spark." *Bookslut*, December 2011.

Mellor, Anne. *Mary Shelley: Her Life, Her Fiction, Her Monsters*. New York: Routledge, 1988.

———. "Reflections on Writing Mary Shelley's Life." In *Mary Wollstonecraft and Mary Shelley: Writing Lives*, edited by Helen M. Buss, D. L. Macdonald, and Anne McWhir, 233–41. Waterloo, Ontario: Wilfrid Laurier University Press, 2001.

Moers, Ellen. *Literary Women: The Great Writers*. New York: Oxford University Press, 1985.

Monroe, Harriet. "Shelley." *Poetry* 20, no. 4 (1922): 206–14.

Mueller, Lisel. *Alive Together*. Baton Rouge: Louisiana State University Press, 1996.

Murray, E. B. Introduction to *Percy Bysshe Shelley Volume IV: A Facsimile of Bodleian MS. Shelley d. 1, part one*. New York: Garland Publishing, 1988.

Nelson, Maggie. *The Argonauts*. Minneapolis: Graywolf Press, 2015.

Nitchie, Elizabeth. *Mary Shelley, Author of "Frankenstein."* New Brunswick, N.J.: Rutgers University Press, 1953.

———. "Mary Shelley's *Mathilda*: An Unpublished Story and Its Biographical Significance." *Studies in Philology* 40 (1943): 447–62.

Penberthy, Jenny. Introduction to *Collected Works*, by Lorine Niedecker. Berkeley: University of California Press, 2002.

Plecas, Jennifer. *BAH! Said the Baby*. New York: Philomel Books, 2015.

Prins, Yopie, and Virginia Jackson. "Lyrical Studies." *Victorian Literature and Culture* 27, no. 2 (1999): 521–30.

Rajan, Tilottama. "Mary Shelley's *Mathilda*: Melancholy and the Political Economy of Romanticism." *Studies in the Novel* 26, no. 2 (1994): 43–68.

Redden, Molly. "Texas Has Highest Maternal Mortality Rate in Developed World, Study Finds." *The Guardian*, August 20, 2016.

Rilke, Rainer Maria. *Selected Poems*. Translated by C. F. MacIntyre. Berkeley: University of California Press, 1940.

Rose, Ellen Cronan. "Custody Battles: Reproducing Knowledge about 'Frankenstein.'" *New Literary History* 26, no. 4 (1995): 808–32.

Rustin, Susanna. "I Lived with Muriel Spark." *The Guardian*, July 5, 2014.

Sedgwick, Eve Kosofsky. *Between Men: English Literature and Male Homosocial Desire*. New York: Columbia University Press, 1985.

Sendak, Maurice. *Where the Wild Things Are*. New York: Harper Collins, 2012.

Seymour, Miranda. *Mary Shelley*. London: John Murray, 2000.

Shelley, Mary. Facsimile of the manuscript draft of Mathilda. *Percy Bysshe Shelley Volume IV: A Facsimile of Bodleian MS. Shelley d. 1, part one*. Edited by E. B. Murray. New York: Garland Publishing, 1988.

———. *Frankenstein*. Edited by D. L. Macdonald and Kathleen Scherf. Peterborough, Ontario: Broadview Editions, 2012.

———. "A History of the Jews." In Jane Blumberg, *Mary Shelley's Early Novels*, 190–202. Iowa City: University of Iowa Press, 1993.

———. *The Journals of Mary Shelley, 1814–1844*. Edited by Paula R. Feldman and Diana Scott-Kilvert. Oxford Scholarly Editions Online, 2015.

———. *The Last Man*. Oxford, Eng.: Oxford World's Classics, 1998.

———. *The Letters of Mary Wollstonecraft Shelley*, vol. 1, edited by Betty T. Bennett. Baltimore, Md.: Johns Hopkins University Press, 1980.

———. *Mathilda*. Brooklyn, N.Y.: Melville House Publishing, 2008.

———. *Mathilda*. Peterborough, Ontario: Broadview Press, 2017.

———. "On Ghosts." In *The Mary Shelley Reader*, edited by Betty T. Bennett and Charles E. Robinson, 334–40. New York: Oxford University Press, 1990.

Shelley, Percy Bysshe. "My Lost William (To William Shelley)." In *The Shelley-Godwin Archive*, MS HM 2177, 46r (rev.). Retrieved from http://shelleygodwinarchive.org/sc/hu/to_william/#/p1.

Siebers, Tobin. "Broken Beauty: Disability and Art Vandalism." *Michigan Quarterly Review* 41, no. 2 (2002): 223–45.

Solnit, Rebecca. *The Faraway Nearby*. New York: Penguin, 2014.

Spark, Muriel. *Mary Shelley*. Manchester, Eng.: Carcanet, 2013.

Spicer, Jack. *The Collected Books of Jack Spicer*. Los Angeles: Black Sparrow Press, 1975.

———. *The House That Jack Built: The Collected Lectures of Jack Spicer*, edited by Peter Gizzi. Middletown, Conn.: Wesleyan University Press, 1998.

Stone, Jon, and Michael Smollen. *The Monster at the End of This Book*. New York: Golden Books, 2003.

Swinburne, Algernon Charles. *Selections from Swinburne*. Edited by H. M. Burton. New York: Cambridge University Press, 1927.

Thorpe, Rufi. "Mother, Writer, Monster, Maid." *Vela*, June 2016. velamag.com

Traister, Rebecca. "Warning: Abortion's Deadly DIY Past Could Soon Become Its Future." *The Cut*, January 10, 2017. www.thecut.com.

Twinn, Michael, and Pam Adams. *LION: A Child's Play Pocket Pal*. Bridgemead, Swindon UK: Child's Play (International) Ltd, 2000.

———. *Pocket Pal PUPPY*. Bridgemead, Swindon UK: Child's Play (International) Ltd, 1995.

Veeder, William. *Mary Shelley and "Frankenstein": The Fate of Androgyny*. Chicago: University of Chicago Press, 1986.

Vickers, Nancy J. "Diana Described: Scattered Woman and Scattered Rhyme." *Critical Inquiry* 8, no. 2 (Winter 1981): 265–79.

Viorst, Judith. *Necessary Losses*. New York: The Free Press, 2002.

White, Newman Ivey. *Shelley*, vol. 2. New York: Alfred A. Knopf, 1940.

Wilson, Elizabeth A. *Gut Feminism*. Durham, N.C.: Duke University Press, 2015.

Winnicott, D. W. *Babies and Their Mothers*. Reading, Pa.: Addison-Wesley Publishing Company, Inc., 1987.

———. *The Child, the Family, and the Outside World*. Reading, Pa.: Perseus Publishing, 1987.

Wollstonecraft, Mary. "The Cave of Fancy." In *The Works of Mary Wollstonecraft*, vol. 1, edited by Janet Todd and Marilyn Butler, 191–206. New York: New York University Press, 1989.

———. *The Collected Letters of Mary Wollstonecraft*. Edited by Janet Todd. New York: Columbia University Press, 2003.

———. *Letters Written in Sweden, Norway, and Denmark*. New York: Oxford University Press, 2009.

———. *"Mary, A Fiction" and "The Wrongs of Woman, or Maria."* Peterborough, Ontario: Broadview Press, 2012.

Youngquist, Paul. "*Frankenstein*: The Mother, the Daughter, and the Monster." *Philological Quarterly* 70, no. 3 (1991): 339–59.

Zagajewski, Adam. *Eternal Enemies*. New York: Farrar, Straus and Giroux, 2008.

INDEX

Page references in **bold** refer to illustrations. The abbreviation MWS refers to Mary Wollstonecraft Shelley.